TAÍNO REVIVAL

Critical Perspectives on Puerto Rican Identity and Cultural Politics

ARLENE DÁVILA

JORGE DUANY

PETER ROBERTS

MIRIAM JIMÉNEZ-ROMÁN

ROBERTO MUCARO BORRERO

TAÍNO REVIVAL

EDITED BY

GABRIEL HASLIP-VIERA

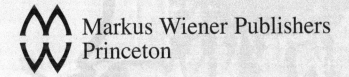

Markus Wiener Publishers
Princeton

Fourth printing, 2019
Copyright © 2001 by Centro de Estudios Puertorriqueños
Hunter College, City University of New York

Cover illustration by Joseph "Doc Sunshine" Leon.
Photos by Arlene Dávila and Holger Thoss

For information write to:
Markus Wiener Publishers
231 Nassau Street, Princeton, NJ 08542
www.markuswiener.com

Library of Congress Cataloging-in-Publication Data

Taíno revival: critical perspectives on Puerto Rican identity and cultural politics/
Gabriel Haslip-Viera, editor.
    Includes bibliographical references.
    ISBN 978-1-55876-258-9 (hardcover : alk. paper)
    ISBN 978-1-55876-259-6 (paperback : alk. paper)
    1. Ethnicity—Puerto Rico.   2. Taino Indians—Ethnic identity.
    3. Identity (Psychology)—Puerto Rico.   4. Nationalism—Puerto Rico.
    5. Puerto Rico—Race relations.
    I. Haslip-Viera, Gabriel.
    F1983.A1 T35 2001
    305.8'0097295—dc21   2001026977

Markus Wiener Publishers books are printed in the United States of America on
acid-free paper,and meet the guidelines for permanence and durabilityof the Committee
on Production Guidelines for Book Longevity of the Council on Library Resources

Table of Contents

Preface

The essays prepared for publication in this volume were originally presented as papers at a symposium titled "Rethinking Taíno: The Cultural Politics of the Use of their Legacy and Imagery," which was held at New York's El Museo del Barrio on February 28, 1998. The symposium, which was organized by anthropologist Arlene Dávila and museum curator Fatima Bercht, was part of a series of events connected to the Museo's art exhibit, "Taíno: Pre-Columbian Art and Culture from the Caribbean." In addition to the presentation of academic papers, the symposium also included a lively and provocative discussion between the conference panelists and a substantial audience that included representatives from various "Taíno" and Native American organizations. Overall, the panelists were highly critical of what has come to be known as the "Taíno revival movement" and its conceptual basis. As a result, a critical assessment of the symposium by Roberto Mucaro Borrero, a representative of the United Confederation of Taíno People has been included in this volume.

The editor wishes to thank the following persons and institutions for their support in facilitating the publication of this volume: Arlene Dávila, Roberto Mucaro Borrero, Markus Wiener, the staff of the City University of New York Center for Puerto Rican, its current director, Dr. Félix Matos Rodríguez, and New York's El Museo del Barrio, its current director, Ms. Susana Torruella Leval, and Ms. Fatima Bercht, curator, for their support in facilitating the publication of this volume.

For other illustrations, see between pages 82 ans 83.

1. Introduction

GABRIEL HASLIP-VIERA

Competing Identities: Taíno Revivalism and other Ethno-racial Identity Movements among Puerto Ricans and other Caribbean Latinos in the United States, 1980–present

As a result of the new, more overt forms of racism and elitism that re-appeared during the Reagan presidency of the 1980s,[1] Puerto Ricans and other Caribbean Latinos revived or developed new concepts of personal and group identity to deal with an economic, social and political environment that became increasingly hostile or indifferent. Government cutbacks in education and social services at the federal, state and local level, and the overall progressive impoverishment of lower middle class and working class people from the early 1980s to the mid-1990s led to increased tensions and conflicts among various groups in U.S. society.[2] Confronted by crime, drugs, homelessness, decreased educational and economic opportunities, and the emergence of political and cultural leaders who called for a halt to immigration, affirmative action, "multiculturalism," "political correct-ness," and "handouts for the poor,"[3] large numbers of Puerto Ricans and other Caribbean Latinos joined various political, religious and cultural organizations in an often desperate attempt to preserve whatever status or dignity they had in U.S. society.

Many became "new born Christians," or joined the Pentecostal Church and other "Protestant" denominations, some of which had also attracted earlier generations of Puerto Ricans and other Latinos with their intensive "spiritualism" and their moral and social discipline.[4] Those who joined these groups generally continued to define themselves by their national or ethnic backgrounds; however, in many instances, a religious identity would become much more important than an identity as a Puerto Rican, Dominican, Cuban, or Latino. In other words, individuals would over-emphasize religious identity and spirituality at the expense of ethnic, racial, or even national identity, with their often negative connotations in U.S. society.[5] However, Puerto Ricans and other Caribbean Latinos also joined other groups, some of them religious, that also acknowledged or emphasized identity by nationality, ethnicity, and race. These groups included urban "youth gangs" that emphasized neighborhood and group solidarity based on nationality, ethnicity and race, such as the Latin Kings and the Ñetas. They also included rival ethno-racial and cultural groups, such as the Afrocentrists, the Nation of Islam, the "Latino Israelites," and the "neo-Taínos," who are the subject of this book.[6]

According to Arlene Dávila, Jorge Klor de Alva and others,[7] the current United States–based Taíno revival movement originated during the period of radical politics and cultural awakening that emerged at the end of the 1960s. However, an interest in the development of a Taíno identity actually began in the Caribbean islands in the middle of the nineteenth century. Starting in the 1840s, the elitist creole advocates for independence in both Cuba and Puerto Rico adopted a mixed Spanish and indigenous identity as part of their effort to separate themselves from the Spanish authorities and their creole loyalists. A mixed or unmixed indigenous identity was also promoted in the Dominican Republic during the same period as part of the effort to separate Dominicans from their despised Haitian neighbors to the west.[8] Antiquarians, novelists, poets, linguists, and historians studied and romanticized the indigenous past, but in the nineteenth century, the pre-Columbian peoples of the Greater Antilles were subdivided by their island localities and referred to not as Taínos, but as "Borincanos" and "Borinqueños" (Puerto Rico), "Siboneyes" (Cuba), "Haitianos" and "Quisqueyanos," (Hispaniola), and "Xamay-quinos" (Jamaica). The term Taíno came into common use only in the early decades of the twentieth century, when scholars such as Antonio Bachiller y Morales, Jesse Walter Fewkes, and M.R. Harrington used the term to refer to the entire indigenous population of the western

Caribbean.[9] The mixed Spanish and indigenous identity of the nineteenth century also became the basis for the official or semi-official tripartite identity of Spanish, Indian, and African that emerged in Cuba and Puerto Rico by the middle of the twentieth century.[10] There was also an ongoing oral tradition on the islands, dating back to at least the early nineteenth century, that focused on an exclusive Taíno pedigree for certain segments of the rural population. In his 1974 book, *The Islands*, Stan Steiner referred to this oral tradition when he focused on a Puerto Rican story-teller or *cuentista* who described an alleged Taíno survivalism in the villages and towns of the mountainous interior of Puerto Rico.[11] It is clear that this storytelling tradition also formed the basis for the emergence of the grassroots Taíno revival movement in the United States and on the islands by the later years of the twentieth century.

The late 1960s and early 1970s were years of political ferment and cultural change throughout the United States. Significant numbers of alienated Puerto Ricans and other Caribbean Latinos in the Northeast and Middle West changed their dietary habits, revitalized Latin music, invented new art forms, and studied Caribbean history and culture.[12] Many of these individuals studied the pre-Columbian Taínos for the first time in their lives during this period. However, others claimed to be "aware" of their Taíno "roots" as a result of stories or *cuentos* they had heard from parents, grandparents, or from other members of their families. Many Puerto Ricans and other Caribbean Latinos became devotees of an idealized Taíno culture. Artists, musicians, poets, and other persons interested in Taíno culture began to establish study groups and other organizations.[13] By the end of the 1980s, a number of Taíno "tribes," "councils," and "associations" had emerged at the grass roots level in various parts of the country. These were connected to other similar groups that had emerged in Puerto Rico and the other islands of the Spanish-speaking Caribbean during the same period. In the early 1990s, they included Nación Taína, Taíno del Norte, the Taíno Intertribal Council of New Jersey, El Consejo General de Taínos Borincanos, Maisití Yucayeque Taíno, and working coalitions or confederations, such as "La Asociación Indígena Taína."[14] In their own specific ways, all of these groups have worked to reclaim or recreate the Taíno language, culture, religion, and an essentialist Taíno identity for their members and other interested persons.

3

For example, there has been the attempt to revive the rituals and the polytheistic religious beliefs of the pre-Columbian Taínos based on archaeological research and the writings of sixteenth-century Spanish chroniclers, such as Ramón Pané and Gonzalo Fernández de Oviedo. There has also been the attempt to recreate the lost Taíno language through the compilation of word lists and the development of a Taíno/English "dictionary." An examination of certain internet websites also reveals the preoccupation with a Taíno pedigree, which is often articulated at the expense of any African, European, or Asian background or ancestry. There is also the focus on the land, the forests, and the indigenous animal life of Puerto Rico, along with environmental concerns and the attempt to recapture the alleged sensitivity that the pre-Columbian Taínos had with regard to the environment.[15]

Some of the cynics among Puerto Ricans and other Caribbean Latinos claim that Taíno revivalism is connected, first and foremost, to a desire for self-enrichment through the acquisition of land and the establishment of gambling casinos, museums, and other profitable enterprises. They point to the establishment of such enterprises on Indian reservations in the continental United States in recent years and their overall success.[16] The cynics also fear that the Taíno revival movement can potentially aggravate racial tensions or conflicts within the Puerto Rican, Cuban, and Dominican communities. However, despite the appeal of the Taíno revival movement to certain individuals, it also has to be recognized that Puerto Ricans and other Caribbean Latinos have been attracted to other groups and associations with competing concepts of culture, religion, ethnicity, and race.

Historically, many Puerto Ricans, Cubans, and Dominicans have been attracted to the ideals of Spanish culture, with its more than occasional emphasis on racial "whiteness" and Eurocentrism. However, *hispanidad*, or the Spanish ideal, has declined among Puerto Ricans and other Caribbean Latinos in the diaspora, to be replaced by other cultural convictions and certainties.[17] For example, a significant but unknown number of Puerto Ricans, Dominicans, and Cubans have become Afrocentrists since the early 1980s. But in contrast to those who have joined the Taíno revival movement, the overwhelming majority of Afrocentrists are not rganized into formal associations or groups at the middle class or grass roots level.

4

In general, most Afrocentrists are individuals who are influenced by the cultural activities and the extensive literature created by Afrocentric scholars, schoolteachers, dilettantes, and artists. It also has to be recognized that there are different kinds or different schools of Afrocentrism. For example, there is an Afrocentrism that merely tries to recapture the neglected African or "black" perspective of world history and culture "through the eyes of black people." But, there also is the much more pervasive racialist Afrocentrism that emphasizes the alleged primacy and superiority of "black people" and "black culture" as opposed to the inferiority of "white people" and other groups.[18]

Puerto Ricans and other Latinos from the Caribbean who become Afrocentrists tend to be persons of darker skin color who are defined as "mulatto," "black," or "African" in appearance. Those who accept the more extreme racialist ideas in Afrocentrism are taught that humanity began in Africa, that the first anatomically modern humans were "black" or "Africoid," and that the early "blacks" migrated from Africa to populate the "Near East," Europe, Asia, Australia, and even the Americas, without undergoing any perceived genetic or biological change between 100,000 and 11,000 years ago.[19] In contrast to the prevailing Neo Taíno belief that all Native Americans miraculously sprang from the soil of the Americas, the Latino Afrocentrists are taught that "invading Mongoloids" began to displace an early "Black" or "Africoid" population by "3200 BC." They are also taught that the "resistant Africoids" were "uprooted," "exterminated," or "almost totally absorbed" by these invaders, and that the "fusion" of these two groups resulted in the emergence of the "American Indian" as a physical or racial type in the centuries that followed.[20]

Afrocentric teaching also emphasizes the "blackness" and primacy of ancient Nile Valley civilizations. The peoples of ancient Egypt and Nubia are said to have created or influenced the creation of *all* the major and minor civilizations of the world, including those of ancient India, China, Southeast Asia, Europe, and the Americas.[21] Again, in the specific case of the Americas, it is claimed that a group of ancient Egyptians and Nubians sailed across the Mediterranean and the Atlantic to the Gulf coast of Mexico around 1200 BC. It is further said that upon their arrival, the Egypto-Nubians came into contact with friendly, but inferior, natives, who willingly accepted them as inspirational pedagogues and rulers. The claim is also made that the new pedagogues and rulers created or inspired the development of the Olmec civilization, which in turn inspired all the other Mesoamerican or Central Mexican civilizations that followed, including those of the Zapotecs in Oáxaca, El Tajín in Veracruz, and the Maya civilization of Guatemala, Honduras, Belize, and the Yucatán.[22]

There is also the assertion that "black Africans" organized other voyages to the Americas in the centuries that followed the alleged first contact. According to the predominant hypothesis, the most important of these voyages was the expedition led by Abu-Bakari II, the West African emperor of medieval Mali, who allegedly sailed across the Atlantic to the Gulf coast of Mexico with a large fleet of ships in 1311 AD. Following the example established in the Egypto-Nubian scenario, the claim is made that Abu-Bakari and his agents influenced the Mixtecs, the early Aztecs, and other peoples of fourteenth-century central Mexico in the areas of economics, technology, religion, and the arts. The Afrocentrists also claim that "Black" Africans had a profound influence on other indigenous groups in North America, the Caribbean, and South America at various times between the twelfth century BC and the fifteenth century AD. In the case of South America, the claim is made that "Black" Africans came into contact and influenced the major complex societies of that continent, such as the Chavín civilization, Tiwanaku, the Chimú, and the Incas. In the case of the Caribbean, and despite Neo Taíno assertions that the pre-Columbian Indians evolved in isolation, the claim is made that West African "merchants" interacted with the pre-Columbian Taínos on a more or less continuous basis after 1311 AD, and that these "merchants" introduced a "Libyan" writing system,[23] and a trade in objects made of gold and copper alloys called "guanin."[24]

For the Latino Afrocentrists who accept these extreme claims, the message is clear (or should be clear). Latino Afrocentrists should self-identify as "black," if they have not done so already. "Black Africans" or "black people" should be seen as culturally and racially superior. "White people" should be seen as racially inferior and their religions and cultural values should be rejected in favor of a polytheistic West African or ancient Egyptian belief system.[25] All Native Americans should be seen as people who are partly "black." These would include the alleged pre-Columbian

6

ancestors of contemporary Neo Taínos, and the indigenous progenitors of modern day Latinos from Mexico, Central America, and South America. All Native Americans should also be seen as slow, dull-witted, unimaginative people who needed the inspiration and the assistance of "black people" from Africa to become "civilized." College instructor Clyde Ahmad Winters summarizes the extreme Afrocentric position best when he states:

> The first civilization to appear in the Americas, called the Olmec culture, was founded by Africans. . . . In addition to teaching the Indians how to grow crops, the (African) Olmecs also taught them how to make calendars and build step pyramids. . . . The original Maya were probably Africans. . . . The Aztecs, Zapotecs, Toltecs and Maya usually occupied urban centers built by Africans, or Afro-Indians. Once the Indians were bound to African colonists for trade goods which they themselves could not produce, they settled in the urban centers where they learned architecture, writing, science and technology from African technicians. As a result, the technology being brought to the Amerindians was of African origin.[26]

In addition to Afrocentrism and the Taíno revival movement, Puerto Ricans and other Caribbean Latinos have also joined Louis Farrakhan's Nation of Islam in recent years. As in the case of the Afrocentrists, most of these individuals are persons of "black," "mulatto," or "African" appearance who have been attracted to the Nation of Islam because of its organizational structure, its regimentation, and its concept of individual responsibility, discipline, and morality.[27] Those who become Black Muslims are also taught to accept an inflexible religious orthodoxy that emphasizes an essentialist view of race based on good versus evil, and a divine prophecy of apocalyptic destruction and survival that can be contrasted to the more tolerant polytheism of the Neo Taínos.[28] According to this dogma, the "Originator" or "Supreme God" (Allah) created the sun, the planets, and the universe from a "triple blackness" ("space, water, and divinity") about seventy trillion years ago.[29] He then created the "original humanity," which was "black," and a council of twenty-four Gods, imams, or "scientists" to help him manage the universe in all its complexity. In the course of time, the original humanity became corrupted and began to separate into two major subgroups—"the happy" and "the dissatisfied." Subsequently, the "Supreme God" called a meeting of his council to discuss the future of humanity and the universe. At this meeting, the council determined that there would be a time of great evil—a time of harshness and suffering that would be necessary to redeem a fallen humanity and create a perfect world.

This time of evil was to begin near the holy city of Mecca among "the dissatisfied" with the birth of Yacub, 8,400 years ago. Yacub grew up to be a "scientist" and an advocate for "the dissatisfied," who preached rebellion against the authorities. Alarmed, the King of Mecca had Yacub and his followers arrested and exiled to the island of "Pelan" or Patmos in the Aegean. In exile, Yacub determined to create a race of "devils" that would enable him and his followers to conquer and terrorize "the original people." Over the course of time, a race of "white devils" lacking "divine substance" was created "through a strict code of birth control" and breeding. The "white devils" were subsequently sent back to "the first civilization" to create mayhem among the "original people"; however, Allah and a group of "strong black warriors" intervened to stop the turmoil. The prophecy was not to be fulfilled at this point. With divine intervention, the "white devils" were rounded up and sent across the Arabian Desert "to the hills and caves of the Caucasus," where they lapsed into a state of savagery for the next two thousand years. In the period that followed, the "white devils" remained in their savage state, "crawled on all fours," ate raw meat—especially pig meat, had no intelligible language, and copulated with animals—especially with dogs, who became their favored pets.[30]

According to the ideology of the Nation of Islam, the next two thousand years continued to be a period of cultural achievement for "the first civilization," which was established in all parts of the world. The "original people" built the pyramids and the Sphinx in Egypt, worshipped the holy Kaaba in Mecca, and excelled in mathematics, philosophy and the arts. However, God also sent Moses (called "Musa") to the Caucasus near the end of this period to fulfill the divine prophecy. Moses instructed the "white devils" in the rudiments of civilization and taught them how to be conquerors and oppressors of the "original people."[31] Allah also put the "original people" into a mental and moral slumber, and in the centuries that followed, the "white devils" began to establish their dominion over the world. The ancient Greeks and Romans, the early modern French, Spaniards, and English, the "imposter Jews,"[32] and the United States (called "Babylon"), were able to establish their rule over Europe, Asia, Africa, and the Americas during this period. However, the rule of the "white devils" is also predicted to end at an opportune moment in the near future. According to the divine prophecy, Allah or the "Supreme God" will bring "Armageddon" to the world and destroy the "white devils" and their mechanisms of oppression and control. Only the most Islamic or "faithful brethren" among the "original people" (those who "wake up") will be able to survive this holocaust. They in turn will join the "Supreme God" and his council of "divine scientists" in the creation of a perfected civilization that will adhere to the moral, ethical, and spiritual principles of the "true" Islam.

It should be noted at this point that the Black Muslim ideology is riddled with contradictory statements and ideas, and has evolved in an ad-hoc fashion over the years.[33] Nevertheless, certain basic principles are easily understood and accepted by Puerto Ricans and other Caribbean Latinos who join the Nation of Islam. In addition to a religion that emphasizes individual responsibility, discipline, submission to Allah, and a strict moral code, there is also the notion that all Puerto Ricans and other Latinos are "black people" or part of the "original humanity." Consequently, there is an inclusiveness to the notion of "blackness" in the ideology of the Nation of Islam. "Black people" include persons who are "brown, red and yellow" as well as "black";[34] but there also is the peculiar view of Native Americans that brings us back to the Afrocentric hypothesis of black African superiority. In contrast to the Neo Taínos, the Black Muslims believe that Native Americans or "Red Indians" are descended from the "Indians" of South Asia who were exiled to the Western Hemisphere as punishment for breaking the laws of Islam 16,000 years ago.[35] The Black Muslims also accept the Afrocentric view that the first civilization of the Americas was created by black Africans (the Olmecs), and that the "Red Indians" learned architecture, writing, science, and technology from African settlers.[36] Again, we are confronted with an extreme concept that emphasizes the racial superiority of black Africans at the expense of those who would emphasize a special identity as Neo Taínos, or Hispanics and other persons of mixed background.

In addition to the Nation of Islam, the Neo Taínos, and the other racial identity groups already described, a number of young Puerto Ricans and other Latinos have become members of a group that could be called the "Latino Israelites." This movement, like Afrocentrism and the Nation of Islam, has its roots in the African-American community, specifically among the "Black Jews" or the "Black Hebrew Israelites" of the northern United States, whose origins can be traced back at least to the 1920s if not earlier.[37] For the Latino Israelites, an autonomous Taíno pedigree is not possible because they see themselves as the "brown" and "black" descendants of the twelve tribes of ancient Israel. Thus, Puerto Ricans are seen as the descendants of "Ephraim," Dominicans are the descendants of "Simeon," Cubans are the descendants of "Manasseh," with African Americans, Native Americans, Jamaicans, Mexicans, Peruvians (etc.) having their own specific origins among the ancient Hebrews.[38]

The "Latino Israelites," like the Black Muslims, the Afrocentrists, and the Taíno revivalists, promote an essentialist view of race, identity, culture, and religion. Quoting passages from the Bible, the "Latino Israelites" see the ancient Hebrews as a persecuted "Black" and "Brown" people who were conquered and dispersed by the ancient Assyrians and Babylonians in the sixth and seventh centuries B.C. In one of their favorite stories, the ancient Israelites are forced to migrate from Palestine to various parts of West Africa, where they eventually settle as pariahs to be sold as slaves to European merchants during the era of the trans-Atlantic slave trade (1450 to 1850 A.D.).[39] This scenario enables the Black and Latino Israelites to distinguish themselves from Asians, Europeans, and Africans of all skin colors in frequently peculiar ways.

For example, Black West Africans are seen as the people who sold the Israelite "ancestors" of African-Americans, West Indians, Puerto Ricans, and other Latin Americans into slavery, and are ardently disparaged. As a "chosen people," the Black and Latino Israelites are also prohibited from mixing with the "vile," "repulsive," "dirty," and "depraved" peoples of Asia, Africa, and Europe. The Europeans and the "imposter" European

Jews are singled out for particular venom because they are seen as evil "red people" or descendants of the devil. In this particular instance, the Black and Latino Israelites can be compared to the Black Muslims with their phobia of "white devils" and "imposter Jews." Like the Nation of Islam, but in contrast to the Neo Taínos, the ideology of the Black and Latino Israelites also includes an apocalyptic future full of vengeance, death, and resurrection. Accordingly, it is predicted that a "black-skinned" Christ with "white bushy hair" will come to earth in the near future to save the Black and Latino Israelites and bring death and destruction to all Asians, Africans, and Europeans throughout the world.[40]

As we have seen in the previous discussion, there are major ideological differences between the "Neo Taínos," the Afrocentrists, the Nation of Islam, and the "Latino Israelites"; however, there are also important similarities that link these groups together. To one degree or another, all of these groups have created and promote an essentialist view of history, culture, race, and religion. For example, the Afrocentrists, the Black Muslims, the Latino Israelites, and the neo-Taínos have created new and self-serving histories for themselves that are partly factual and partly contrived.[41] They appropriate, recreate, or invent new cultural and religious "traditions" that are partly based on historical folkways and beliefs.[42] They also promote, in one way or another, revised concepts of race and ethnicity that are based on ideas first developed by Europeans in the sixteenth century.[43]

In the case of the Neo Taínos and the Afrocentrists, the Judeo-Christian-Islamic religious tradition is minimized, ignored, or disparaged in favor of a revived or recreated religious polytheism or "spiritual philosophy" based on pre-Columbian Caribbean, West African, and ancient Egyptian belief systems.[44] In the case of the Nation of Islam and the Latino Israelites, the Judeo-Christian-Islamic tradition is distorted, reinterpreted, and racialized to root out "white devils," "imposter Jews," "dirty" Africans, and other undesirables. In all of these cases, there is a reinterpretation, critique, or rejection of any cultural or religious idea or belief that has any connection with Europeans or "white people." Santería and other Caribbean religious syncretisms, which are important to many Afrocentrists, provide us with good examples of this exclusionist position. Caribbean Santería, Voodoo, Obeah, and other related belief systems are the product of a centuries-old religious tradition that combines Christianity with the traditional polytheistic cults of West Africa. Santería in the Spanish-speaking Caribbean may also include some minor elements that can be traced to the religious belief systems of the pre-Columbian Taínos and "Caribs."[45] In any case, there is the tendency within Afrocentrism to minimize, reinterpret, or ignore the European and Native American components in favor of the African influences or elements in Santería and other Caribbean syncretisms.[46] At the same time, those who become Afrocentrists are encouraged to adopt the traditional West African cults or the ancient Egyptian polytheism that is favored by the extremists in the Afrocentric movement.[47]

Essentialist race concepts also characterize all of these groups. To one degree or another, the Neo Taínos, the Afrocentrists, the Nation of Islam, and the Latino Israelites have adopted the traditional European and Anglo-American race concepts in revised form to suit their purposes. "Black" people, Native Americans, and other "people of color" are seen as warm, open, civilized, and hospitable "sun people," while Europeans and European-descended persons are seen as cold, unscrupulous, calculating, and destructive "devils" or "ice people."[48] Utilizing the traditional "one drop rule" of racial classification adopted by Europeans and Anglo-Americans in the nineteenth century,[49] persons of "mixed race" or even persons of European background can be categorized as "Blacks," "Israelites," or Native Americans. In the case of the Taíno revivalists, this may mean that persons of "white" or European appearance with black or dark brown hair may be accepted as Native Americans or Taínos.[50] However, it is not clear that persons of "black" or "mulatto" appearance with tightly coiled hair and skin color that is light to medium brown would customarily be accepted as Taínos because of their alleged "African" looks.[51]

In general, all of these groups have taken economic, social, and political positions that can be described as conservative, accommodationist, or non-threatening to the prevailing social order. In the early years of its development, the Nation of Islam was seen as a subversive group that could potentially threaten the social stability of the United States and its government. Local law enforcement agents and the Federal Bureau of Investigation under J. Edgar Hoover harassed the Nation of Islam throughout the decade of the 1930s. During the Second World War, the Black Muslim leader, Elijah Muhammad, was jailed for draft evasion and alleged collaboration with agents of the Japanese. There were also the efforts to establish a "separate state or territory" for the Nation of Islam "on this continent or elsewhere" in the late 1960s and early 1970s—an idea also attributed to contemporary Neo Taínos. However, since the mid-1970s, the Nation of Islam has emphasized economic self-development, the recruitment of new members, and preparation for the coming Armageddon, which is also the major concern of the Black and Latino Israelites.[52]

In contrast to the other groups, the Taíno revivalists have been much more involved in protests and advocacy work. The Neo-Taínos have been active on environmental issues and on issues involving the rights of all Native Americans. They have participated in events sponsored by various national and international organizations, such as the annual "International Day of the World's Indigenous Peoples," which is sponsored by the United Nations. They also have lobbied for the release of Leonard Peltier, the Anishinabe-Lakota "political prisoner" falsely accused of murdering two FBI agents in 1975.[53] But despite these and other similar activities, the Neo Taínos should not be seen as political radicals or as radical reformers. Their fixation on the "revival" of the Taíno language, culture, and lifestyle clearly demonstrates their overall accommodationist and politically conservative orientation. The same can also be said of the Afrocentrists, who are clearly preoccupied with racial identity, psychology, ancient history, and Afrocentric self-development and morality to the exclusion of other issues or concerns.[54]

Although there are similarities between the Taíno revivalists, the Afrocentrists, the Nation of Islam, and the Latino Israelites, their potential growth and ideological competitiveness create the capacity for increased social and cultural fragmentation within the already sub-divided African-American, Puerto Rican, and Caribbean communities. This tendency towards social and cultural fragmentation and re-fragmentation is not all that unusual and can be seen in all multicultural societies and political systems that have evolved throughout history, along with attempts at cultural integration and homogenization.[55] In general, relations between the Neo-Taínos, the Afrocentrists, the Black Muslims, and the

Latino Israelites, and relations between these groups and other groups are characteristically tenuous or non-existent despite the rhetoric of some of their leaders. For example, Louis Farrakhan, the head of the Nation of Islam for the past twenty-eight years, has expressed sympathy or support for the Colombian and Salvadoran rebels, the Sandinistas of Nicaragua, and Fidel Castro and the Cuban revolution. However, this largely empty rhetoric has not been connected to any real activism or advocacy work. There also has been no connection or relationship between the Nation of Islam and any of the more important Latino organizations in the United States, despite an articulated support for these groups.[56] By contrast, Farrakhan's predecessor, Elijah Muhammad, was suspicious of Fidel Castro, the Cuban revolution, and any other group that had connections to communism and the former Soviet Union. In the early 1960s, Muhammad came to the conclusion that Castro was a "white devil" because of his appearance and his connections to the Russians. However, unlike Farrakhan, Muhammad entered into agreements with militant Native American, Latino, and African-American activist groups that were ideologically different at a time in the late 1960s when agencies of the United States government were actively trying to create conflicts among these groups.[57]

Farrakhan and the Nation of Islam have also expressed support for the Black Hebrew Israelites and the Afrocentrists.[58] The Nation of Islam has incorporated Afrocentric ideas into its ideology,[59] and accepts the Hebrew Israelites as part of the "original" humanity; however, it appears that the Black and Latino Israelites and the Afrocentrists have maintained their distance from the Nation of Islam because of significant ideological differences that are seen as irreconcilable. Indeed, many Afrocentrists tend to disparage Farrakhan and the Black Muslims for their acceptance of a religious belief system that is seen as alien to Africans and has justified the Islamic slave trade and "Arab" oppression of Black people since the eighth century AD.[60] By contrast, the Afrocentrists tend to tolerate or accept the Black Hebrew Israelites because of their alleged ancient origins and connections with the ancient Egyptians and Nubians. Indeed, Dr Yosef Ben-Jochannan, a Black Hebrew Israelite, who claims to be Puerto Rican, is considered one of the premier Afrocentric scholars.[61] Nevertheless, the Afrocentrists have also been cautioned about establishing intimate links with persons who do not identify as black or African, such as (presumably) the Neo Taínos, and other Latinos and diasporans who emphasize a Native American or mixed racial heritage based on geographic or national origin.[62] The Afrocentric view of this issue has been summarized by Temple University professor Molefi Asante, who notes that:

> Of all the continents, Africa had often seemed the most disconcerted by its children who have been scattered over the globe. A great part of this has to do with the confusion of the children of Africa themselves. Often detached and isolated from Africa they assume new identities and become doubly lost zombies in the midst of stone and steel cities of the Americas. Yet it is imperative that the African in Colombia who speaks Spanish, (and) the African in Brazil who speaks Portuguese . . . be brought into this (Afrocentric) cultural project . . . . Just as the Australian European living thousands of miles away from Europe participates in the European project; the African must be brought into the (Afrocentric) cultural project of Africa whether in Cuba or the United States . . . Nicaragua, Mexico or Colombia.[63]

Because the current Taíno revival movement is of relatively recent vintage, the Neo Taínos have had little or no meaningful contact with the Afrocentrists, the Nation of Islam, or the Latino Israelites as organized groups. For the most part, the Neo Taínos have concentrated their attention on cultural self-development and the establishment of links with other Native American groups in the United States and throughout Latin America and the Caribbean. Important ideological differences of an obvious nature also separate the Neo-Taínos from the Afrocentrists, the Black Muslims, and the Latino Israelites. At this point, a systematic study of these groups is needed to determine their actual size and influence among Puerto Ricans and other Caribbean Latinos. At the same time, it is clear that all of these groups are competing for the attention of young alienated Puerto Ricans and other Latinos in the Caribbean, and especially in the mainland communities of the United States. For the most part, Puerto

Ricans and other Caribbean Latinos of part or "noticeably African" background or "appearance" have been attracted to the ideas of the Afrocentrists, the Nation of Islam, and the "Latino Israelites." At the same time, Puerto Ricans, Cubans, and Dominicans with a stereotypically "Indian" or European "appearance" have become "Israelites" or Taínos.[64] Thus, the Taíno revival movement should not be seen as a peculiarly aberrant or isolated experience. It should be seen as part of a much larger phenomenon in which disaffected or alienated individuals are attracted to alternative cultures and lifestyles because of prejudice, discrimination, poor living conditions, and severely limited economic and social opportunities, among other factors. Thus, in the United States, the increased popularity of the Taíno revival movement can be compared to the increased popularity of other generally similar phenomena. These include, in addition to those already mentioned, the "New Age" movement, the Church of Scientology, the "Promise Keepers," the "Five Percenters," the Norse revival movement, "Los Mitas" (in Puerto Rico), and other movements of this type.

Notes

1. See Bernstein (1994), Henry (1994), Herrnstein and Murray (1994), Lynn (1989, 1991), Rushton (1995), and Sowell (1981, 1984) among others for writings that reflect the new forms of elitism and racism that first emerged in the early 1980s. Reference also should be made to the racialist writings of Arthur R. Jensen and William Shockley, published in the late 1960s and early 1970s, which continued to be popular in the 1980s and 1990s, with Jensen still active up until the present time. See Jensen (1969, 1998) and Pearson (1992).

2. On government cutbacks and the increasingly hostile social and economic climate for poor people in the 1980s and early 1990s, see Gans (1995), Katz (1989), Quadagno (1994), and Piven and Cloward (1997) among other works.

3. The politically conservative or reactionary views towards immigration, affirmative action, "multiculturalism," and "political correctness" were articulated in the 1980s and 1990s by Bennett (1992), Brimelow (1995), Duignan and Gann (1995), Glazer (1975), Murray (1984), and Schlesinger (1991) among others.

4. On the Pentecostal church and Latino involvement in other Protestant or evangelical denominations, see Anderson (1979), Díaz Stevens and Stevens-

Arroyo (1998), Pérez y González (2000: 145–147), and Poblete and O'Dea (1960).

5. Nominally Roman Catholics for the most part, Puerto Ricans and other Latinos from the Caribbean have also become Jews, Mormons, Buddhists, and orthodox Muslims, or they have joined other religious denominations. However, the numbers converting to these faiths appear to be relatively small in comparison to those who have become Pentecostalists or evangelical Christians.

6. For a discussion of the creation of ethnic and national identities and the issue of their authenticity, see Anderson (1991), Chatterjee (1993), Handler and Linnekin (1984), and Linnekin (1991) among other works. For a discussion of this issue as it pertained to Mexican-Americans and Puerto Ricans in the United States in the 1970s, see Klor de Alva (1997).

7. See Dávila, pp. 40–41, 42–43 in this book, and Klor de Alva (1997).

8. See Roberts (1997) and Schmidt-Nowara (2001). Also see Dávila, p. 37, and Duany, pp. 58, 62–65 in this book.

9. Schmidt-Nowara (2001).

10. See Dávila, pp. 37–38, and Duany, pp. 58–60, 62–65 in this book.

11. Steiner (1974: 7–19).

12. See Center for Puerto Rican Studies (1974), López (1973), Young Lords Party (1971), Klor de Alva (1997: 66–71 and passim), and the relevant chapters in Flores (1993, 2000) and Torres and Velázquez (1998). Also, see Dávila, pp. 40–41, 42–43 in this book.

13. See Dávila, pp. 34–35, 40–41, in this book.

14. See Dávila, p. 18 in this book. Reference also should be made to the creation in 1998 of the United Confederation of Taíno People, a new broad-based coalition of tribal groups, which still functions up until the present time. See United Confederation of Taíno People (1998).

15. See various articles in *La Voz del Pueblo Taíno*, the newsletter of the United Confederation of Taíno People. There are also statements and articles on various internet websites, such as "Presencía Taína" (2001), "Taíno Inter-Tribal Council" (2001), "Jatibonicu Taíno Tribal Nation" (2001), and the "Caribbean Amerindian Centrelink" (2001). Also, see the articles by Dávila and Jiménez Román in this book for comments on the essentialist nature of Neo-Taíno identity.

At this point, reference should also be made to recent claims that the "mitochondrial DNA" of "Taínos" has been found in two sample groups of Puerto Ricans studied by Juan Carlos Martínez Cruzado, a biology professor at the Mayaguez campus of the University of Puerto Rico. Although these claims have been summarized in newspaper reports in an exaggerated or sensationalized manner, Dr. Martínez Cruzado has not come to the conclusion that pureblooded Taínos or Native Americans can be found in the contemporary Puerto Rican population. In an on-going study, Martínez Cruzado and a team of researchers expect to find genetic material that is mostly African and "Caucasian" in the "Y-chromosomes" of Puerto Ricans, which is passed through the male line, as opposed to the mitochondrial DNA, which is passed "exclusively" through the female line. Given the controversial nature of the preliminary findings, the research of Martínez Cruzado and his team also needs to be subjected to a rigorous peer review process in a scientific journal. Historical evidence also strongly suggests that most of the Taíno population of Puerto Rico was wiped out by the 1530s or 1550s. Consideration also needs to be given to the migration (forced or otherwise) of Native Americans, Mestizos, and Mulatos with Native American ancestry, who came to Puerto Rico from the Bahamas, Venezuela, Mexico, and other parts of the Caribbean and Latin America from 1500 to 1900. On the genetic research project and its preliminary findings, see Martínez Cruzado (2000). Also see *The San Juan Star* (April 18, 1999), *El Nuevo Día* (July 11, 1999), and *El San Juan Star* (August 22, 1999) for the sensationalized reports of "Taíno DNA." On the movement of Native Americans and persons of mixed background with Native American ancestry to the Spanish-speaking Caribbean during the periods 1492–1550 and 1763–1808, see Anderson Córdova (1990: 218–275, 303–318), Haslip-Viera (1999: 111–112), and Pike (1983: 134–147 and passim).

16. See, for example, the Associated Press (2000).

17. At the present time, most active hispanophiles and their organizations are found in the Spanish-speaking Caribbean and other parts of Latin America, as opposed to the United States mainland.

18. On the different types of Afrocentrism, see Karenga (1993: 35), Marable (1993: 120–122 and passim), Walters (1991), and Wiley III (1991: 1, 20–21).

19. See Brunson (1988), Diop (1991), Clegg (1992), Rashidi and Brunson (1988), among others. Also, see Howe (1998) for a comprehensive critique of Afrocentrism and its various claims.

20. Clegg (1992), Rashidi (1992), and Van Sertima (1992: 23–24). For a critique of this hypothesis, see Haslip-Viera (1996), which has been revised and updat-

ed for re-publication in the near future.

21. See Browder (1992), Diop (1991), Van Sertima, ed. (1985, 1992), and Van Sertima and Rashidi, eds. (1988), among other works.

22. See Van Sertima (1976, 1995, 1998) and the relevant essays in Van Sertima, ed. (1992).

23. In this case, Van Sertima is making highly controversial claims about the well-known pre-Columbian Taíno and Carib pictographs carved in stone and other materials. For examples and a discussion of these pictographs, see Fewkes (1970: 148–159 and plates LX, LXI), Martínez Torres (1981), Pagán Perdomo (1978), and Priego (1977: 163, 166, 166, 168–171).

24. Van Sertima (1976, 1995, 1998) and the relevant essays in Van Sertima, ed. (1992). For a critique of the ideas articulated by Van Sertima and the other Afrocentrists who support or supplement his ideas, see Haslip-Viera, Ortíz de Montellano and Barbour (1997), Howe (1998: 249–251, 257), Ortíz de Montellano, Haslip-Viera and Barbour (1997), and Ortíz de Montellano (2000a, 2000b).

25. See Asante (1988), Carruthers (1995), and Karenga (1989, 1990, 1993), in addition to Browder, Brunson, Legrand Clegg, Diop, Rashidi, Van Sertima and others.

26. Winters (1981–1982).

27. Numerous books and articles have been published on the Nation of Islam over the years. The most important recent publications are those of Andrew Clegg (1997), Evanzz (1999), and Gardell (1996).

28. From a historical standpoint, all or most polytheistic religions (as belief systems) have been generally tolerant and accommodating—often incorporating new ideas and elements from other religions that may result in syncretisms. The polytheism of the Neo Taínos seems to reflect this historical reality; however, proselytizing religions, such as Christianity and Islam, with their rigid and inflexible orthodoxies, have been generally intolerant of other religions and beliefs. See Ferguson (1970: pp. 211–243 and passim); MacMullen (1981: 1–5 and passim), and Wilken (1984), among other works, for a discussion of this issue as it pertained to the Mediterranean world in late antiquity. Also see the comments by Roberto Mucaro Borrero on the Neo-Taíno view towards religion and religious tolerance in note 44 of this essay.

29. The synopsis of the Black Muslim religious ideology that follows is based on Gardell (1996: 144–186 and passim), Clegg (1997: 41–73 and passim), and Evanzz (1999: 74–80 and passim).

30. In a speech titled "The Origin of the White Race: The Making of the Devil" that was delivered at the Maryam Mosque in Chicago on April 23, 1989, Louis Farrakhan asked the following, which is quoted in Gardell (1996: 152, 434):

    Who is the [white] man's best friend?
    You?
    No—the dog.
    He and the dog had a love affair.

31. According to Gardell (1996: 152), the Nation of Islam uses the following passage from Genesis 1:28 in the Bible as proof of this assertion:

    And God said . . . be fruitful and multiply, and replenish the earth, and subdue it: and have dominion over the fish of the sea, and over the fowl of the air, and over every living thing that moveth upon the earth.

    It should be noted that adherents of the Nation of Islam consider the Bible a "poison book." See Clegg (1997: 56).

32. In recent years, "white Jews" have been vilified by the Nation of Islam as "devils" and "imposters" who appropriated the religious and cultural heritage of the ancient Israelites or "Black Jews" (seen as a branch of the "original people"). See Nation of Islam, Historical Research Department (1991). According to Clegg and Gardell, the European Jews were not vilified in this way by the Nation of Islam in the early years of its development. See Clegg (1997: 53, 54) and Gardell (1996: 267–269 and passim).

33. The best discussion of this issue is found in Gardell (1996: 165–174 and passim).

34. Gardell (1996: 159). For other references to the Black Muslim view that all non-"whites" are "black," see Gardell (1996: 335–336, 359 note 80).

35. Gardell (1996: 153). In his book, *Message to the Blackman*, Nation of Islam leader Elijah Muhammad (1965: 107) referred to Native Americans as the "Red Lost and Found Nation of Islam." See Gardell (1996: 376 n.56). Also, see Clegg (1997: 47–48) for a somewhat different discussion of this issue.

36. Gardell (1996: 152–153).

37. On the history of the "Black Jews" or "Black Hebrew Israelites" of the United States, see Brotz (1970), Chireau (2000), Moses (1982), and Wynia (1994).

38. The other nationalities and their alleged tribal origins are as follows: African Americans/Judah, West Indians/Benjamin, Haitians/Levi, Central Americans/Zebulon, North American Indians/Gad, Seminole Indians/Reuben, "Argentina to Chile"/Napthali, "Columbia (sic) to Uruguay"/Asher, with Mexicans connected to Issachar (from flyer in author's possession). It also should be noted that Brazil, the Guianas, Surinam, and Venezuela are missing from the list, and that the "Black Jews" based in New York are currently divided into three or four different factions, with at least one group articulating a rhetoric that rejects the notion that Latinos and Native Americans can be Israelites. On the different factions, see "General Description of the Black Jewish or Hebrew Israelite Community" in Ben Levy (2001).

39. This information is derived from "Nuestra Cultura Verdadera," a series of programs that was shown on public access television in New York City from February 20, 1995 to June 17, 1996 (videotapes in author's possession). For a somewhat different but very long and confused version of this story, see Malcioln (1996).

40. This information is derived from a specific program in the series "Nuestra Cultura Verdadera" which was shown on August 21, 1995 (videotape in author's possession).

41. For the Afrocentrists, published examples of these works include Diop (1991), Jackson (1970), James (1976), Van Sertima (1976), and Williams (1987). For the Nation of Islam, they include Muhammad (1965, 1973) and Nation of Islam, Historical Research Department (1991). For the Black Hebrew Israelites, they include Ben Jochannan (1983), Malcioln (1996), and Moses (1982: 183–195). For the Taíno revivalists, see the internet websites for Presencia Taína (2001), the Taíno Inter-Tribal Council (2001), the Jatibonicu Taíno Tribal Nation (2001), and Caribbean Amerindian Centrelink (2001). The reader is also encouraged to visit the internet websites of the Mexican-American "Aztlanistas," who have also articulated ideas with regard to Native American identities that are comparable to those of the Taíno revivalists. These include Aztlán México Nation (2001) and the Chicano Mexicano México Empowerment Committee (2001).

42. In the case of the Taíno revivalists, see various statements or comments on their internet websites. For the Afrocentrists, see the sections on "Kwanza" in Karenga (1993: 173–174, 202) and "Njia: The Way" in Asante (1988: 109–120). For the invented ad-hoc cultural and religious tradition of the Nation of Islam, see the summaries in Clegg (1997), Evanzz (1999), and Gardell (1996).

43. For a recent discussion and critique of the Afrocentric views on race, see

Howe (1998: 265–286 and passim). On the racialist ideas of the Nation of Islam and the Taíno revivalists, see the relevant sections in Clegg (1997), Evanzz (1999), Gardell (1996), and the essays by Dávila and Jiménez Román in this book.

44. According to Borrero (2001), the Táino revivalists are tolerant of all faiths and promote traditional Native American "spiritualism" and the acceptance of Christian/Native American syncretisms. However, there also is a fear of the rigid intolerance of the Catholic Church, and anxiety about the growing influence of Evangelical Christians and other dogmatic groups, such as the Mormons. In the case of the Afrocentrists, the Judeo-Christian-Islamic tradition is frequently subjected to an intense critique that often leads to rejection; however, Molefi Asante, the guru of the Afrocentric movement, sees Christian churches as potential vehicles for the spread of Afrocentric beliefs and the downgrading or elimination of Christianity. See Asante (1988: 2–6, 7, 47, 48; 71–78; 1990: 61, 62, 115–116, 130; 1993: 65–75). Also see Usry and Keener (1996) for an Afrocentric Christian critique of anti-Christian Afrocentrists, such as Asante.

45. On Santería in the Caribbean and the United States mainland, see Brandon (1993), González-Wippler (1982), Murphy (1993), and Pérez y Mena (1991).

46. In a self-serving way, the Black Muslims ignore the fact that persons defined as "white" are active devotees of Santería, and may even function as leaders in Santería cults. By contrast, the Latino Israelites may redefine these "whites" as "Israelites" if they are people who originate or come from Latin American and the Caribbean.

47. There seems to be a tendency on the part of some Neo-Taínos and several Afrocentric "scholars" to view the traditional belief systems as "spiritual," "sacred," or "guiding" philosophies, as opposed to religions or religious cults. See Asante (1988: 21–24, 109–123 and passim), Carruthers (1995) and Karenga (1989, 1990). This view has also been articulated for the Taíno revivalists by Borrero (2001).

48. It should be noted here that these descriptors have been used by the Nation of Islam, the Black and Latino Israelites, and the extremists among Afrocentrists, such as Leonard Jeffries of the City College of New York, who first used the terms "sun people" and "ice people" to describe Europeans or European-descended persons. By contrast, the Taíno revivalists, although very critical of the role that Europeans have played throughout history, do not use the more extreme terminology. On Leonard Jeffries, see Dyson (1992), Howe (1998: 221–222 and passim), and Morrow (1991).

49. The "one drop rule" refers to the principle or belief that "black people," by definition, are persons who have at least "one drop of black blood." For an extensive discussion of this concept, see Davis (1991) and Malcomson (2000).

50. Taíno chief Peter Guanikeyu Torres and Taíno "storyteller" Bobby González are two individuals in the Taíno revival movement who could easily pass for Europeans or European-descended "white" persons if they were to change their grooming habits and adopt standard European and Anglo-American clothing.

51. See Dávila, pp. 45–46 and Jiménez Román, pp. 124–126 in this book.

52. For the Nation of Islam, see the relevant sections in Clegg (1997), Evanzz (1999), and Gardell (1996).

53. See various articles in the newsletter *La Voz del Pueblo Taino* in Taíno Inter-Tribal Council (2001).

54. The critique by the quasi-Marxist political historian, Manning Marable, has been particularly scathing in this regard. According to Marable (1993: 118–119):

> The black nationalist-oriented-intelligentsia, tied to elements of the new African-American upper middle class by income, social position and cultural outlook, began to search for ways of expressing itself through the "permanent" prism of race, while rationalizing its relatively privileged class position.

Marable (1995: 200) also notes that the Afrocentrist:

> looks to a romantic, mythical reconstruction of yesterday to find some understanding of the cultural basis of today's racial and class challenges. Yet that critical understanding of reality cannot begin with an examination of the lives of Egyptian Pharoahs. It must begin by critiquing the vast structure of power and privilege which characterizes the political economy of post-industrial capitalist America.

55. In addition to the United States, historical and modern examples of structured multicultural societies and political systems include the ancient Persian or "Achaemenid" empire, the ancient "Mauryan" empire of South Asia, Ptolemaic Egypt, the Roman empire, the nineteenth-century Austro-Hungarian empire, modern Nigeria, the former Soviet Union, and the former Yugoslavia.

56. Gardell (1996: 5, 205, 283, 287).

57. Clegg (1997: 156), Evanzz (1999: 221–223, 332). At the present time, Minister Muhammad Abdullah (a.k.a. Diógenes Rodríguez), a native of the Dominican Republic, is the designated national representative of the Nation of Islam for Latin America and Latinos living in the United States. It is not clear, however, what impact Mr. Abdullah is having on NOI relations with Latinos aside from his advocacy work for Afro-Latino civil rights and his attempt to recruit members for the Nation of Islam. Mr. Abdullah is also a member of the Organization of Africans in the Americas, but this group is a peculiar amalgam of individuals that include Afrocentrists, interested academics, advocates for Afro-Latinos, and persons connected to private corporations and agencies of the United States government.

58. Gardell (1996: 152–153, 269). At this point in time, there is no clarity on whether Farrakhan is aware of the existence of the Neo-Taínos and the Latino faction of the Hebrew Israelites, or whether he would see these groups as being worthy of attention.

59. See the Afrocentric ideas that are incorporated into Nation of Islam, Historical Research Department (1991).

60. Howe (1998: 234–235, 282). It also should be noted that despite his scathing criticism of "Arabs" and the Islamic religion, Molefi Asante has praised Elijah Muhammad as an effective organizer and inspirational figure. See Asante (1988: 14–15, 20, 48). Also see (1998: 2–6, 48; 1990: 61, 62, 115–116, 130; 1993: 65–75) for Asante's critique of Islam and the "Arabs."

61. For a reference to Ben-Jochannan's alleged Puerto Rican background, see Howe (1998: 226, 228–229 note 13). According to Howe, Ben-Jochannan has two Spanish middle names, "Alfredo" and "Antonio," and claims to have been active in the New York–based movement for Puerto Rican independence. He also notes that Ben Jochannan's first recorded publication was written in Spanish. See Howe (1998: 228–229 note 13). Georgina Falú (2000), a Puerto Rican Afrocentrist, also claims a Puerto Rican pedigree for Ben-Jochannan.

62. Reference to this issue is made by Rodríguez (1996: 146).

63. Asante (1988: 106).

64. It is true that quite a number of stereotypically "African"-looking Caribbean Latinos may see themselves not as "blacks," but as Native Americans or Taínos. However, this phenomenon is largely limited to persons from the Dominican Republic and its diaspora. During the era of the Rafael Trujillo dictatorship (1930–1961) and at various times before and up until the present,

a Native American pedigree has been imposed or encouraged by the Dominican elites and the government for all Dominicans of "non-white" appearance in an effort to separate the mostly mulatto population from the despised Haitians to the west. For a discussion of this issue, see Duany (1998: 153 and passim), Roberts (1997), and Torres Saillant (1998).

References

Anderson, Benedict. 1991. *Imagined Communities: Reflections on the Origins and Spread of Nationalism*. London: Verso.

Anderson, Robert Mapes. 1979. *Vision of the Disinherited: The Making of American Pentecostalism*. New York: Oxford University Press.

Anderson-Córdova, Karen Frances. 1990. *Hispaniola and Puerto Rico: Indian Acculturation and Heterogeneity, 1492-1550*. Ph.D. dissertation, Yale University.

Asante, Molefi Kete. 1988. *Afrocentricity*. Trenton, N.J.: Africa World Press.

———. 1990. *Kemet, Afrocentricity and Knowledge*. Trenton, N.J.: Africa World Press.

———. 1993. *Malcolm X as Cultural Hero and other Afrocentric Essays*. Trenton, N.J.: Africa World Press.

Associated Press, 2000. "Reservations With Casinos Gain Ground On Poverty," *New York Times* (September 3, Section 1): 19.

Aztlán Mexica Nation. 2001. <http://www.dickshovel.com/Isab.html>.

Ben Jochannan, Yosef. 1983. *We the Black Jews: witness to the "white Jewish race" Myth*. New York: Alkebu-lan Books.

Ben Levy, Rabbi Sholomo. 2001. <http://www.columbia.edu/~sbl7/bjewl.html> (printout in author's possession).

Bennett, William J. 1992. *The De-Valuing of America: The Fight for Our Culture and Our Children*. New York: Summit Books.

Bernstein, Richard. 1994. *Dictatorship of Virtue: Multiculturalism and the Battle for America's Future*. New York: Alfred A. Knopf.

Borrero, Roberto Mucaro. 2001. Personal communication, 5 January.

Brandon, George. 1993. *Santería from Africa to the New World: The Dead Sell Their Memories*. Bloomington: Indiana University Press.

Brimelow, Peter. 1995. *Alien Nation: Common Sense About America's Immigration Disaster*. New York: Random House.

Brotz, Howard. 1970. *The Black Jews of Harlem; Negro nationalism and the dilemmas of negro leadership*. New York: Schocken Books.

Browder, Anthony T. 1992. *Nile Valley Contributions to Civilization*. Washington, D.C.: Institute of Karmic Guidance.

Brunson, James. 1992. "African Presence in Early China," in *African Presence in Early Asia,* Ivan Van Sertima and Runoko Rashidi, eds., pp. 120–137. New Brunswick, N.J.: Transaction Publishers.

Caribbean Amerindian Centrelink. 2001. <http://members.nbci.com/cariblink/index.html>

Carruthers, Jacob. 1995. *Mdw Ntr, Divine Speech: A Historiographical Reflection of African Deep Thought from the Time of the Pharaohs to the Present.* London: Karnak House.

Center for Puerto Rican Studies. 1974. *Centro taller de cultura: conferencia de historiografia.* New York: Centro de Estudios Puertorriqueños.

Chatterjee, Partha. 1993. *The Nation and Its Fragments: Colonial and Post Colonial Histories.* Princeton: Princeton University Press.

Chicano Mexicano Mexica Empowerment Committee. 2001. <http://www.mexica-movement.org/frames.html>

Chireau, Yvonne. 2000. *Black Zion: African American Religious Encounters with Judaism.* New York: Oxford University Press.

Clegg, Claude Andrew III. 1997. *An Original Man: The Life and Times of Elijah Muhammad.* New York: St. Martin's Press.

Clegg, Legrand II. 1992 [1979]. "The First Americans," in *African Presence in Early America,* Ivan Van Sertima, ed., pp. 231–240. New Brunswick, N.J.: Transaction Publishers.

Davis, F. James. 1991. *Who is Black?: One Nation's Definition.* University Park: Pennsylvania University Press.

Díaz-Stevens, Ana María, and Antonio M. Stevens-Arroyo. 1998. *Recognizing the Latino Resurgence in U.S. Religion: The Emmaus Paradigm.* Boulder, Colorado: Westview Press.

Diop, Cheikh Anta. 1991. *Civilization or Barbarism: An Authentic Anthropology.* Chicago: Lawrence Hill Books.

Duany, Jorge. 1998. "Reconstructing Racial Identity: Ethnicity, Color, and Class among Dominicans in the United States and Puerto Rico," *Latin American Perspective,* 25 (3): 147–172.

Duignan, Peter, and Lewis H. Gann. 1995. *Political Correctness: A Critique.* Stanford, California: Hoover Institution Press.

Dyson, Michael Eric. 1992. "Melanin Madness," *Emerge,* 3: 4 (February): 32–34, 36–37.

Evanzz, Karl. 1999. *The Messenger: The Rise and Fall of Elijah Muhammad.* New York: Pantheon Books.

Falú, Georgina. 2000. Statement made at the symposium on "Afro-Latinos and the Issue of Race in the New Millennium," Brooklyn College, City University of New York, 21 October.

Ferguson, John. 1970. *The Religions of the Roman Empire.* Ithaca, N.Y.: Cornell University Press.

Fewkes, Jesse Walter. 1970 [1907]. *The Aborigines of Porto Rico and Neighboring Islands.* New York: Johnson Printing Company.

Flores, Juan. 1993. *Divided Borders: Essays on Puerto Rican Identity.* Houston: Arte Publico Press.

_____. 2000. *From Bomba to Hip-Hop: Puerto Rican Culture and Latino Identity.* New York: Columbia University Press.

Gans, Herbert J. 1995. *The War on the Poor: The Underclass and Antipoverty Policy.* New York: Basic Books.

Gardell, Mattias. 1996. *In the Name of Elijah Muhammad. Louis Farrakhan and the Nation of Islam.* Durham, N.C.: Duke University Press.

Glazer, Nathan. 1975. *Affirmative Discrimination: Ethnic Inequality and Public Policy.* New York: Basic Books.

González-Wippler, Migene. 1982. *The Santería Experience.* Englewood Cliffs, N.J.: Prentice Hall.

Handler, Richard, and Jocelyn Linnekin. 1984. "Tradition, Genuine or Spurious," *Journal of American Folklore,* 97 (385): 273–290.

Haslip-Viera, Gabriel. 1996. "Afrocentrism and the Peopling of the Americas," *Ethnic Studies Review,* 19 (2–3): 129–140.

——. 1999. *Crime and Punishment in Late Colonial Mexico City, 1692–1810.* Albuquerque: University of New Mexico Press.

Haslip-Viera, Gabriel, Bernard Ortíz de Montellano, and Warren Barbour. 1997. "Robbing Native American Cultures: Van Sertima's Afrocentricity and the Olmecs," *Current Anthropology,* 38 (3): 419–441.

Henry, William A. 1994. *In Defense of Elitism.* New York: Doubleday.

Herrnstein, Richard J., and Charles Murray. 1994. *The Bell Curve: Intelligence and Class Structure in American Life.* New York: The Free Press.

Howe, Stephen. 1998. *Afrocentricity: Mythical Pasts and Imagined Homes.* London: Verso.

Jackson, John G. 1970. *Introduction to African Civilizations.* New York: University Books.

James, George. 1976 [1954]. *Stolen Legacy.* San Francisco: Julian Richardson Associates.

Jatibonicu Taíno Tribal Nation. 2001 <www.members.dandy.net-orocobix/index.html>

Jensen, Arthur R. 1969. "How Much Can We Boost IQ and Scholastic Achievement?" *Harvard Educational Review* 39 (1): 1–123.

——. 1998. *The g factor.* Westport, Connecticut: Praeger.

Karenga, Maulana. 1989. *Selections from the Husia: Sacred Wisdom of Ancient Egypt,* 2nd Edition. Los Angeles: University of Sankore Press.

——. 1990. *The Book of Coming Forth by Day: The Ethics of the Declarations of Innocence.* Los Angeles: University of Sankore Press.

————. 1993. *Introduction to Black Studies*. Los Angeles: University of Sankore Press.

Katz, Michael B. 1989. *The Undeserving Poor: From the War on Poverty to the War on Welfare*. New York: Pantheon Books.

Klor de Alva, J. Jorge. 1997. "The Invention of Ethnic Origins and the Negotiation of Latino Identity, 1969–1981," in *Challenging Fronteras: Structuring Latina and Latino Lives in the U.S.* Mary Romero, Pierrette Hondagneu-Sotelo, and Vilma Ortíz, eds., pp. 55–74. New York: Routledge.

Linnekin, Jocelyn. 1991. "Cultural Invention and the Dilemma of Authenticity," *American Anthropologist* 93 (2): 446–449.

López, Alfredo. 1973. *The Puerto Rican Papers: Notes on the Re-Emergence of a Nation*. New York: Bobbs-Merrill.

Lynn, Richard. 1989. "Positive Correlations Between Head Size and IQ," *British Journal of Educational Psychology* (59): 372–377.

————. 1991. "The Evolution of Racial Differences in Intelligence," *Mankind Quarterly* (32): 99–121.

MacMullen, Ramsay. 1981. *Paganism in the Roman Empire*. New Haven, Conn.: Yale University Press.

Malcioln, José V. 1996. *The African Origins of Modern Judaism: From Hebrews to Jews*. Trenton, N.J.: African World Press.

Malcomson, Scott L. 2000. *One Drop of Black Blood: The American Misadventure of Race*. New York: Farrar, Straus and Giroux.

Marable, Manning. 1993. "Beyond Racial Identity Politics: Towards a Liberation Theory for Multicultural Democracy," *Race and Class* 35 (1): 113–130.

————. 1995. *Beyond Black and White: Transforming African-American Politics*. London: Verso.

Martínez Cruzado, Juan Carlos. 2000. "Profiles," *Delaware Review of Latin American Studies* 1 (2): <www.udel.edu/LASP/vol1-2MartinezC.html> (printout in author's possession).

Martínez Torres, Roberto. 1981. *Pinturas Indigenas de Boriquen*. Morovis, P.R.: Ediciones El Mapa.

Morrow, Lance. 1991. "The Provocative Professor," *Time* (26 August): 19–20.

Moses, Wilson Jeremiah. 1982. *Black Messiahs and Uncle Toms: Social and Literary Manipulations of a Religious Myth*. University Park: Pennsylvania State University Press.

Muhammad, Elijah. 1965. *Message to the Blackman in America*. Chicago: Muhammad's Temple of Islam, no. 2.

————. 1973. *The Fall of America*. Chicago: Muhammad's Temple of Islam, no. 2.

Murray, Charles. 1984. *Losing Ground: American Social Policy, 1950–1980*. New York: Basic Books.

Murphy, Joseph M. 1993. *Santería: African Spirits in America.* Boston: Beacon Press.

Nación Taína. 1999. <http://members.aol.com/-ht-a/NaTaina/index.html> (printout in author's possession).

Nation of Islam, Historical Research Department. 1991. *The Secret Relationship between Blacks and Jews.* Chicago: Nation of Islam.

Ortíz de Montellano, Bernard R. 2000a. "'Black Warrior Dynasts:' L'afrocentrisme et le Nouveau Monde," in *Afrocentrismes: L'histoire des Africains entre Égypte et Amérique,* François-Xavier Fauvelle-Aymar, Jean-Pierre Chrétien, and Claude-Hélène Perrot, eds., pp. 249–270. Paris: Éditions Karthala.

———. 2000b. "Early America Revisted. Ivan Van Sertima," *Latin American Antiquity,* 11 (2):195–196.

Ortíz de Montellano, Bernard R., Gabriel Haslip-Viera and Warren Barbour. 1997. "They Were NOT Here before Columbus: Afrocentric Hyperdiffusionism in the 1990s," *Ethnohistory,* 44 (2): 199–234.

Pagán Perdomo, Dato. 1978. *Nuevas pictografías en la isla de Santo Domingo: las cuevas de Borbón.* Santo Domingo: Museo del Hombre Dominicano.

Pearson, Roger, ed. 1992. *Schockley on Eugenics and Race: The Application of Science to the Solution of Human Problems.* Washington, D.C.: Scott Townsend Publishers.

Pérez y González, María E. 2000. *Puerto Ricans in the United States.* Westport, Connecticut: Greenwood Press.

Pérez y Mena, Andrés Isidoro. 1991. *Speaking with the Dead: Development of Afro-Latino Religion Among Puerto Ricans in the United States, A Study into the Interpretation of Civilizations in the New World.* New York: AMS Press.

Pike, Ruth. 1983. *Penal Servitude in Early Modern Spain.* Madison: University of Wisconsin Press.

Piven, Frances Fox and Richard A. Cloward. 1997. *The Breaking of the American Social Compact.* New York: The Free Press.

Poblete, Renato and Thomas F. O'Dea. 1960. "Anomie and the Quest for Community: The Formation of Sects among Puerto Ricans in New York," *American Catholic Sociological Review,* 21 (Spring): 18–36.

Presencia Taína. 2001. <http://www.presenciataina.net/>

Priego, Joaquín, R. 1977. *Cultura Taina* (Third edition). Santo Domingo: Publicaciones America.

Quadagno, Jill. 1994. *The Color of Welfare: How Racism Undermined the War on Poverty.* New York: Oxford University Press.

Rashidi, Runoko, and James Brunson. 1988. "People of the First World: Small Blacks in Africa and Asia," in *African Presence in Early Asia,* Ivan Van Sertima and Runoko Rashidi, eds., pp. 159–162. New Brunswick, N.J.: Transaction Publishers.

Roberts, Peter. 1997. "The (Re)Construction of the Concept of 'Indio' in the National Identities of Cuba, the Dominican Republic, and Puerto Rico," in *Caribe 2000: definiciones, identitades y culturas regionales y/o nacionales,* Lowell Fiet and Janette Becerra, eds., pp. 99–120. Rio Piedras: Facultad de Humanidades, Universidad de Puerto Rico.

Rodríguez, Christopher. 1996. *Latino Manifesto: A Critique of the Race Debate in the US Latino Community.* Columbia, Maryland: Cimarron Publishing.

Rushton, J. Philippe. 1995. *Race, Evolution and Behavior. A Life History Perspective.* New Brunswick, N.J.: Transaction Publishers.

Schlesinger, Arthur M. 1991. *The Disuniting of America.* New York: W.W. Norton.

Schmidt-Nowara, Christopher. 2001. "Conquering Categories: The Problem of Prehistory in Nineteenth-Century Puerto Rico and Cuba," *Centro Journal,* 12 (2): forthcoming.

Sowell, Thomas. 1981. *Ethnic America: A History.* New York: Basic Books.

––––––. 1984. *Civil Rights: Rhetoric or Reality?* New York: William Morrow.

Steiner, Stan. 1975 [1974]. *The Islands: the Worlds of the Puerto Ricans.* New York: Harper Colophon.

Taíno Inter-Tribal Council. 2001. <http://www.hartford-hwp.com/taino/> (print-out in author's possession).

Torres, Andrés, and José E. Velázquez. 1998. *The Puerto Rican Movement: Voices from the Diaspora.* Philadelphia: Temple University Press.

Torres-Saillant, Silvio. 1998. "The Trials and Tribulations of Blackness: Stages in Dominican Racial Identity," *Latin American Perspectives,* 25 (3): 126–146.

United Confederation of Taíno People. 1998. "Declaration of the United Confederation of Taíno People Finalized on January 3, 1998," *La Voz del Pueblo Taino,* 1 (1): 1–2 (also in Taíno Inter-Tribal Council [2001]).

Usry, Glenn and Craig S. Keener. 1996. *Black Man's Religion: Can Christianity be Afrocentric?* Downers Grove, Illinois: InterVarsity Press.

Van Sertima, Ivan. 1976. *They Came Before Columbus: The African Presence in Ancient America.* New York: Random House.

––––––. 1992. "Fifteen Years Later [An Introduction and Overview]," in *African Presence in Early America,* Ivan Van Sertima, ed., pp. 5–27. New Brunswick, N.J.: Transaction Publishers.

––––––. 1995. "African Presence in Early America," in *Race Discourse, and the Origins of the Americas: A New World View,* Vera L. Hyatt and Rex Nettleford, eds., pp. 66–101. Washington, D.C.: Smithsonian Institution Press.

––––––. 1998. *Early America Revisited.* New Brunswick, N.J.: Transaction Publishers.

Van Sertima, Ivan, ed. 1985. *African Presence in Early Europe.* New Brunswick, N.J.: Transaction Publishers.

––––––. 1992. *African Presence in Early America.* New Brunswick, N.J.: Transaction Publishers.

Van Sertima, Ivan, and Runoko Rashidi, eds. 1988. *African Presence in Early Asia.* New Brunswick, N.J.: Transaction Publishers.

Walters, Ronald. 1991. "A Different View: 'Afrocentrism' Means Providing the Neglected Black Perspective," *American Educator*, 15 (3): 26–27.

Wiley III, Ed. 1991. "Afrocentrism: Many Things to Many People," *Black Issues in Higher Education*, 8 (17): 1, 20–21.

Wilken, Robert L. 1984. *The Christians as the Romans Saw Them.* New Haven, Conn.: Yale University Press.

Williams, Chancellor. 1987 [1974]. *The Destruction of Black Civilization: Great Issues of a Race from 4500 B.C. to 2000 A.D.* Chicago: Third World Press.

Winters, Clyde Ahmad. 1981–1982. "Mexico's Black Heritage," *The Black Collegian* (December–January): 76–84.

Wynia, Elly M. 1994. *The Church of God and Saints of Christ: The Rise of the Black Jews.* New York: Garland Press.

Young Lords Party and Michael Abramson. 1971. *Palante: The Young Lords Party.* New York: McGraw-Hill.

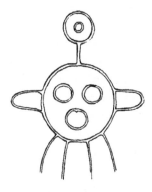

2.

ARLENE DÁVILA

*Local/Diasporic Taínos: Towards a Cultural Politics of Memory, Reality and Imagery**

> And the prophecy said that after 500 years, there will be a resurgence, and that Taínos will reemerge once again. It is like a buried time capsule that's been unearthed. And people will begin to remember and say "hey, we are still here!"
>
> *Aura Surey's Prophesy as told by Naniki Reyes Ocasio*

After a meeting at New York's El Museo del Barrio where I was invited to help contextualize the resurgence of Taíno identity, I was surprised to learn that some Taínos at the meeting had thought me to be also Taíno. As the curator explained afterwards, some were convinced that I too was Taíno, although I had yet to realize it, questioning at once the certainty of my Puerto Rican identity and bringing to the forefront their view that, for many Puerto Ricans, Taíno is a dormant yet realizable identity.

This was not the first time that I had been linked to the Taíno, the pre-Columbian indigenous population that once inhabited the Caribbean, but are now largely presumed to be extinct since the 18th century. During my previous research on cultural politics in Puerto Rico, Francisco Arriví,

*This essay was prepared for a symposium that I was asked to organized as part of the exhibition "Taíno Pre-Columbian Art and Culture from the Caribbean" at El Museo del Barrio in New York City (September 27, 1997–March 1998). I want to thank the staff of El Museo del Barrio, the other panelists who participated in the symposium, and Gabriel Haslip-Viera for coordinating the publication of this collection. Most of all, however, I want to thank the Taínos who kindly shared their time and provided valuable feedback for this work.

one of the island's foremost intellectuals involved in the development of Puerto Rico's national cultural policy, had asked permission to check my front teeth for the "diente de pala" or "shovel shaped front teeth"—a tooth formation thought common among Taínos. That day, I refused to be "examined" by Arrivi, unconcerned about the veracity of this supposedly racial mark of "Taínoness." I remember, however, feeling somewhat perplexed at discovering that one of the key figures involved in developing Puerto Rico's blending myth of nationality, and thus in erasing the indigenous and the African components of Puerto Rican culture as living legacies, would simultaneously believe he could identify a Taíno through something as real and concrete as someone's front teeth.

At El Museo, however, the suggestion was not only that I "looked" Taíno or had Taíno background, but rather that I was denying mine for not identifying myself in this manner. The unstated implications were significant. I had been implicitly accused of being trapped in the old Puerto Rican nationalist canon, the same one that had created new memories out of forgetting, and the same one that promoted the harmonious integration of African, Indian, and Spanish elements into a "whitened" Puerto Rican culture unable to recall its non-Hispanic ancestry. I also had felt the uneasy discomfort of having had my identity questioned outright, which is in fact what contemporary Taínos encounter from a skeptical public on a daily basis. These issues confronted me at once with the contradictions embedded in an easy dismissal of the current resurgence of Taíno identity, even when I have yet to identify myself as anything other than a "Puerto Rican." Such a dismissal does not explain the pervasive appeal of Taíno as a symbol of Puerto Rican identity, or my own ambivalent feelings about my so-called Taíno look. It also does not explain the fear and amusement caused by the current Taíno affirmation and revival among Puerto Ricans in the States and on the island, or the unending interest by my Puerto Rican students in writing and reading about the Taíno, which I myself experienced after first moving to the mainland.

Back then, this interest had led me to write about the historical development of the Taíno as a symbol of Puerto Rico's national identity and to discuss the use and relevance of Taíno for politicians, artists, and the wider public at the level of popular culture. Today, however, the Taíno is no longer a symbol but a living reality. In 1990, The Asociación Indígena

Taína was founded in New York and there has since been a resurgence of groups claiming Taíno descent through a range of means, including blood ties, spiritual descent or commitment to furthering Taíno interests both in the States and on the island. Some of these groups have even made inroads into official circles. The Taíno Tribal Council of Jatibonicu has obtained recognition from the New Jersey Commission on Indian Affairs, while Taíno groups like the Consejo General de Taínos Borincanos have obtained legitimacy through institutions, such as the United Nations League of Sovereign Indigenous Nations.[1] In another example, El Museo del Barrio not only featured a Taíno legacy component into their exhibition on "Taíno Pre-Columbian Art and Culture from the Caribbean" (September 27, 1997–March 1998), but it also recognized the Taínos' legitimate authority over Taíno issues by incorporating them as consultants into the organization and preparation of the exhibit.

Thus, we might ask, is the Taíno resurgence the result of a direct continuity with the past, or is it a New Age fad or a curiosity to be laughed at? Also, does the Taíno resurgence represent a daring oppositional blow to the canons of the blending myth of Puerto Rican nationality, or is it better seen as yet another example of Puerto Ricans' inability to deal with their long subordinate African legacy? This chapter is an attempt to grapple with these complex understandings and rationalizations of this movement and of its implication and potential value for Puerto Rican cultural politics both in the States and on the island. Before engaging on these issues, however, I should note that my objective here is neither to ascertain the veracity or authenticity of Taíno identity nor to define what constitutes its "true" content and definition. Research on the creation of social and ethnic identities has amply shown that issues of authenticity are always fraught with contention and that it is not so much the contents of a given identity as the contexts and purposes for which they are deployed that are most meaningful and revealing (Handler & Linnekin 1984; Linnekin 1991).

Indeed, the defining elements of Taíno identity are very much contested both within and outside the Taíno community and, by themselves, do not explain the growth of this movement or the strong reactions it generates and continues to trigger. My purpose will thus be to provide a discussion of the diverse objectives and goals for which Taínoness has been deployed in order to suggest that the debate over Taíno is not only about the content and nature of this identity, but rather about issues of cultural authority and the role of cultural memory in the very redefinition of Puerto Ricanness both on the island and in the diaspora. In this way, rather than focusing on the "content" of this identity, my analysis probes into the uses of memory, defined here as an active realm of social practice integrating elements of remembrance, history, fantasy, and invention (Sturken 1997: 259). As argued by Sturken and others, it is by recasting memory in this manner that we can move away from the futile, and often problematic linkage of memory and truth to analyze instead the multiple processes through which the past is actively deployed in the present (Ibid; Rowe and Schelling 1991).

My discussion will begin with a brief review of the different contexts in which the Taíno has been mobilized or manipulated in Puerto Rico to provide a background to this revival in the contemporary context. In this section, I will probe particularly the historical role of this indigenous population as a symbol of Puerto Rican national identity since the nineteenth century as well as discuss the governmental appropriation of the Taíno for the conceptualization of a socially and racially balanced Puerto Rican society. I then continue with a discussion of the present manifestation of Taíno identity in New York City, where the movement for Taíno revival has been most directly spearheaded since the 1990s. Finally, my conclusion considers some of the different claims being made through the rubric of Taíno identity and their various implications for the conceptualization of a local and diasporic Puerto Rican identity.

From Symbol to Living Reality:
Perspectives from Here and There

No discourse on Taíno continuity and survival can veil the reality of genocide and mass extermination to which the Taíno were subjected during the Spanish colonization of the island. Accordingly, most anthropological and historical accounts conclude that the Taíno disappeared totally or were absorbed into the Puerto Rican population by the 18th century. The 1778 census provides the last mention of *Indios* as a distinct group (Brau 1978 [1907]), while the manipulation of census figures by the Spanish, and Taíno disappearance from official figures makes it difficult to assess the possibility of their survival after the eighteenth century (Henige 1991; Knight 1990).

What remains unquestioned, however, is the total erasure of this group along with the earliest constructions of national identity by the island's national elite in the nineteenth century. Such a development would consolidate the transmutation of the Taíno from a recognized group and a living population into a symbol to be revived, romanticized and manipulated. This is evident in nineteenth-century literary production, such as in Daniel Rivera's *Agueybana the Brave*, Eugenio de Hostos' *The Pilgrimage of Bayoan*, and Alejandro Tapia-Rivera's *The Cacique's Palm*, which featured Taíno Indians as principal characters to convey messages of national assertion and opposition to the Spanish authorities. In particular, the Taíno, the only non-transplanted population on the island, becomes a conduit of patriotic devotion and a tool to affirm a legitimate and continuous connection to the soil by the Creole "Puerto Rican" elite vis-à-vis the Spanish colonial authorities. The treatment of the Taíno as a long-lost heritage in the nineteenth century is further displayed in the growing interest in Taíno material culture. This interest is evidenced in the first public expositions of Taíno objects in 1854, which were part of the Agricultural and Technology Festival-Exposition, organized by Governor Fernando de Norzagaray, and in the "Museo Militar," founded in November 1854, where Taíno objects were exhibited as "cherished souvenirs of the past"—reaffirming their long-gone status alongside Spanish military paraphernalia (Alegría 1974; Coll y Toste 1968 [1916]).

It is in the twentieth century, however, that the rendering of the Taíno into an object and a symbol would reach its greatest importance. This is evident in the literary production of what is known as the "1930s generation" revolving around the quest for a distinct Puerto Rican nationality, and most directly in the cultural policies of the Pro-Commonwealth government in the 1950s. As has been amply noticed, the 1930s literary production often centered the issue of Puerto Rican nationality on the morality and spiritual superiority of Puerto Rico's Spanish legacy in contrast to the "lack of culture" of the new colonizer—the American invader (Gelpi 1993; Flores 1979). As such, this view not only emphasized the legacy of the previous colonizer, but also simultaneously devalued Puerto Rico's indigenous and African cultural components, which were either minimized or connected with the "weakening" of Puerto Rico's character and culture (Flores 1979). The devaluation of the Taíno and African legacies, however, simultaneously involved the creation and consolidation of meanings about these subverted components. In Antonio Pedreira's classic work *Insularismo*, for instance, the Taíno's contribution to Puerto Rican culture is not only minimized but also associated with a tradition of passivity and compliance—a view that continues to be recycled, although in the guises of goodness and nobility, up to the present day. Thus, among other venues, the view of Taíno culture as a noble and generous legacy has since been reproduced in the government's cultural policy—in films like *The Good Heritage* produced by Puerto Rico's Division of Community Education in the 1950s, as well as in most elementary school textbooks.

With the cultural nationalist policies of the commonwealth in the 1950s, Taíno symbolism was further manipulated through its presentation, alongside the Spanish and African legacies, as "equal" foundational elements of Puerto Rican culture. As I have noted elsewhere, such a presentation was central to the ideal of a harmonious racial and social integration communicated in governmental institutions, such as the Institute of Puerto Rican Culture and its programs. The Institute's seal, for instance, depicts the three racial/ethnic strands (Taíno, Spaniard, and African) next to each other, whereas its program articulates ideas about the putative contribution of each ethnic strand to Puerto Rican culture (Dávila 1997). Accordingly, the Taíno's legacy was folklorized and associated with particular musical instruments, such as the gourd or "guiro," or with traditions such as basket weaving, or with national celebrations, such as in the annual Indigenous Festival in Jayuya involving a massive display of Taíno dress, music, dance, and customs.

Of course, the overt recognition of the Taíno as a contributing element to the national culture does not equate with its equal treatment and evaluation against the other constitutive ethnic components. Although considered superior to the African element (the "third root" and "the last to contribute"), the Taíno influence has always remained subordinate to Spanish culture, to which the most valuable crafts, musical forms, and traditions, from wood "santos" to the *trova*, are traced. In this way, without engaging in a greater discussion of the differential evaluations of the three ethnic and racial strands in Puerto Rican culture, I suggest that the popularity of the Taíno should be analyzed in relation to its historical utility as a mediating symbol between the dominant Spanish and the subordinate African tradition. This role has imbued anything Taíno with implications for issues of race in Puerto Rico, where an Indian legacy remains a vivid referent, a racial buffer, and a basis for claims for racial integration and equality—despite the ongoing reality of racial discrimination directed at "blackness" and things African on the island. Indeed, it is exactly because the Indian heritage has historically received greater attention and public acknowledgment in the government's cultural policy in contrast to what is African, that the emphasis on the Taíno and things Taíno remains contradictory and problematic both for Puerto Ricans in the states and on the island. After all, we have yet to celebrate Puerto Rico's African legacy in everyday life in such a way that it goes beyond the folklorized formula of "festivals of bomba y plena," or to witness a movement of Puerto Rican black consciousness similar to that prompted by the Taíno.

Yet it would be equally problematic to dismiss the political importance of the Taíno because of its historical appropriation by the government's cultural policy and its position within Puerto Rico's racial discourse and hierarchies. For the Taíno has not only been used to project a racially harmonious society but also to voice a variety of political claims, including debating the very political status of the island. We may recall the anti-colonial critiques embedded in the debate among Puerto Rican anthropologists and social scientists in the 1970s over the dominant portrayal of the Taíno as a noble, good but ultimately docile and conquered figure. Such a portrayal of the Taíno in the government's cultural and educational policies was seen as a by-product of the colonial biases that have dominated Puerto Rico's historical interpretations, which aimed at producing the image of a subservient Taíno that fits in with the island's political situation (Maldonado-Denis 1969; Silén 1973; Sued-Badillo 1978).[2] As such, this debate was as much about the Taíno's image as it was about Puerto Rico's political situation. The island's continued association with the United States was connected to a legacy of passivity and compliance that was traced to the Taíno, while at the same time, Puerto Rico's hope for independence was connected to the presentation of the Taíno, not as docile but as active historic figures in their own right.

At the level of popular culture, the Taíno has also been continuously deployed for a variety of goals, as I myself was able to witness during my previous research on the island. It is common to see people dress Taíno or wear T-shirts with Taíno iconography and paraphernalia in public protests and demonstrations. Claiming a Taíno legacy for new and old traditions is always a sure way for people to establish their legitimacy and continuity on the island.

As a general rule, however, it has been the concept of the Taíno rather than a living reality that has been historically deployed for political purposes on the island. As such, the political mobilization of Taíno imagery has never been directed at the canons of Puerto Rico's nationalist ideology, which sees the Taíno as an extinct entity of which only traces and tinges remain. Here lies the greatest difference between the historical use of Taíno symbolism and the current revival of the Taíno as a living heritage demanding recognition in its own right. Before discussing this development, however, let us first turn to New York and the United States mainland, where the Taíno has obtained greater recognition as a realizable living legacy and identity than on the island.

The first thing that should be noted is that although the Taíno has also been employed as a symbol of national identity in New York and the Diaspora, this role has been most of all directed at enhancing the status of a minority group through assertions of cultural distinctiveness. Specifically, the Taíno has been more closely connected to social movements and grassroots activism in the United States than on the island, where the Taíno has had a long history of appropriation by nationalist elites and cultural institutions. The central role of Taíno symbolism in grassroots activism in the United States context is evident in the cultural struggles waged by Puerto Ricans in the 1960s, when Taíno symbolism became a permanent feature in the work of artists and cultural activists (Klor de Alva 1997). Artists like those at El Taller Boricua, for instance, incorporated Taíno imagery in their work and in their posters produced for other activists groups, from the Young Lords to the Movement for Puerto Rican Independence (Dimas 1990). A Taíno pictograph decorated the first logo for El Museo del Barrio, marking its close connection with the struggles of Puerto Rican activists for representation in U.S. society in the 1960s and 1970s (Moreno 1997). Similarly, Taíno themes and pictographs have since adorned the works of a variety of Puerto Rican artists in New York, such as Marcos Dimas, Fernando Salicrup, Nitza Tufiño, and Juan Sánchez, who juxtapose Taíno pictographs with the Puerto Rican flag and other nationalist symbols in paintings developing the themes of nationhood and independence.

Yet in the United States, interest in the Taíno has not been limited to its use as a symbol of assertion but rather was concomitantly developed into an organized movement of ethnic revival intent on rescuing and restoring the Taíno language, culture, and religion. That is, while there are a variety of groups and individuals who identify themselves as Taíno on the island, it has nevertheless been in the United States, particularly in New York City, from which the revival of Taíno identity has been most boisterously assertive since the 1990s. In fact, it was in New York that the first Taíno institutionalized organization, the Asociación Indígena Taína, and one of the largest Taíno political organizations, the Nación Taína, were founded in the early 1990s.[3]

This relatively greater development of the Taíno movement on the mainland is, of course, not surprising considering the current dominance of the discourse on multiculturalism in the United States and its likely impact on the rapid development and manifestation of Taíno identity. Whereas on the island, the nationalist discourse promotes that "we are all Puerto Rican," veiling the subordinate status of sectors of the population according to race and limiting the recognition of distinct groups among "Puerto Ricans." In the United States, the discourse of multiculturalism has afforded greater opportunities for the recognition of the Taíno as a distinct entity. Consequently, the Taíno movement and identity has received greater attention, acceptance, and recognition in the United States than it has on the island, which has yet to afford a comparable public recognition of their existence and revival.

The continental backdrop of the Taíno movement became evident during the aforementioned organizational meeting for the living legacy component of the Taíno exhibition at El Museo del Barrio. This meeting gathered for the first time some important Taíno leaders and activists, a Taíno "Dream Team" as described by a participant, to discuss the current

41

revival, providing a unique entry point into the movement's origins.[4] There, it was evident that whereas the Taínos identified themselves as indigenous from either Boriquen, Quisqueya, or Cubanakán (the indigenous names of Puerto Rico, the Dominican Republic, and Cuba, respectively), most of them had either migrated to the U.S. during their early youth or were born and raised in the U.S. It was also evident from the discussions that it was in the United States that most of the Taínos recouped their indigenous identity. Their memory of their Taíno past, and thus their ability to pro- mote their identity, was in some cases directly instilled by experiences in the United States. For some, it was triggered by their experiences with the Native American movement. For instance, four of the Taíno activists had been involved in this movement, on and off, since the late 1970s, either working on the important Native American Indian publication *Akwesane Notes*, or serving as translators to Central and South American indigenous delegations to the United Nations, or just participating in Native American pow-wows or activities. Accordingly, these experiences gave them a level of acceptance and served as a motivation for their self-identi- fication as Taínos in the years that followed. For, as some argued, Native Americans seemed to know more about their own identity than they them- selves had been allowed to discover prior to their encounter with the Native American movement—prompting them, as one said, to go beyond the confines of traditional categories such as "country" and "place of ori- gin" to inquire about who made up their "people."

Another factor contributing to Taíno self-discovery was their common experience of prejudice, discrimination, and dislocation in U.S. society. Not surprisingly these experiences had instilled in them a "longing to con- nect" and discover their "real identity," part and parcel of their simultane- ous rejection of their imposed and debased status as "Puerto Ricans" or "Hispanics." Thus, it is not at all surprising that it would be the island's rural past, far from the city's urban center that would provide the central reservoir of Taíno memory and heritage. In fact, while many Taínos traced their self-discovery to spiritual inspiration, or to something that was born inside of them, or to memories transmitted by their parents and grandpar- ents, all of them, to a greater or lesser extent, stressed the importance of learning and discovering their rural background as a key medium to their Taíno ancestry. It is the memories and stories transmitted by their rural parents and grandparents that was most stressed as the conduit of Taíno identity. Thus, it was the lifestyle and the material life of the peasant, be it Cuba's *Guajiro*, the Dominican *campesino,* or Puerto Rico's *Jíbaro*, that was consistently presented as a primary conduit for the preservation of Taíno culture and legacy. References to a "Taíno mountain jíbaro culture" by Taíno activists provide an example of the ongoing conflation of peasant and Taíno culture.

The interesting irony here is that the peasant *Jíbaro* culture has traditionally been regarded as the stronghold of the Spanish legacy and of the whitening processes of *mestizaje* in Puerto Rico's nationalist ideology and thus directly implicated in "forgetting" the African and Indian constituent elements of Puerto Rican culture. The re-signification of the peasant as Taíno thus provides the evidence, not only of the constitutive processes of memory and forgetting (Sturken 1997), but also of the endurance and embedded possibilities of that which is "forgotten" (Lipsitz 1991). Specifically, these elements were simultaneously rendered as materials for future appropriation because that which needed to be forgotten was nevertheless constitutive of the dominant myth of nationality, highlighting what Lipsitz terms the "volatile instabilities sedimented within seemingly stable narratives of nation and race" (1997: 326). Accordingly, Taínos are not so much re-interpreting the dominant myth of rurality as wresting its embedded potential by reclaiming it as their "original domain."

The Taíno in the Intersection of Local and Diasporic Puerto Rican Cultural Politics

By now it should be evident that the resurgence of Taíno identity is full of implications that are specific to the diverse contexts in which they take place, be they on the island or in the diaspora. This, by itself, renders an examination of the revival and of its varied implications an elusive and difficult task. Nevertheless I would like to consider some issues that have been the subject of contention and debate and that I believe are of great consequence for Puerto Rican cultural politics in the states and on the island.

43

First, I should clarify that my interest in cultural politics rather than "politics" is deliberate. Most Taínos do not see their movement as a political movement, but rather as a cultural or spiritual one, even though their goals and programs are in fact very much imbued with politics, as will be evident in the discussion that follows. Furthermore, the great diversity among the groups and their cultural and spiritual objectives also hinders any analysis of the political implications of their programs and objectives. Some emphasize the reconstruction of language and traditions, or the study and dissemination of Taíno folktales and artistic forms of expression, whereas there is a great contention about the issue of Taíno spirituality and what are its major components. Others, by contrast, are more concerned with environmental protection and the preservation of the island's natural resources. There are also groups that have advanced specific political demands for the recognition of their movement by state structures and institutions.[5] But, there are also certain commonalities in the way these groups have been organized and the manner in which they project their identity and goals to the public that are worth considering in relation to Puerto Rican cultural politics on the island and in the diaspora.

A key issue is the very assertion of the existence of Taíno ethnicity. As was stated, this claim has been the subject of criticism and skepticism by many, who see this movement as a "New Age" fad or as a crazy invention of "uprooted" Puerto Ricans in the diaspora. Most importantly, this claim has triggered criticisms from Puerto Rican intellectuals who point to the racist implications of the Taíno resurgence—given that, as said before, it is Puerto Rico's African legacy that remains most subverted and subject to racism both in the states and on the island.[6] As a result, by now, most Taínos are well aware that, for many, their identity is one they have "selected" primarily as an escape from their "blackness" and their African past.

Indeed, the resurgence of the Taíno is fraught with contentions about issues of race and authenticity, which seem to reproduce rather than challenge racist discourses and hierarchies. However, this is so not solely because the emphasis on the Taíno may contribute to the further diminution of the African contribution to Puerto Rican culture, as is most commonly thought, but also because racial hierarchies are intrinsic to any dis-

44

course on identity or authenticity. Specifically, while at the level of discourse, contemporary Taínos are in fact quite open about their mixed status and about the reality of racial mixing, racial features are nevertheless a determinant of the individual's Taíno ancestry or "blood," with the "Taíno look" fixed as straight hair, a narrow forehead, elongated eyes, "*chata*" (short) nose, pronounced cheekbones, copper coloring, and lack of body hair, remaining key authenticating elements of Tainoness.

Such a correlation between racial markers and ethnic identity is, of course, not exclusive to the Taíno movement. Instead, it is a development common to most cultural and nationalist movements, resulting from the reproduction of dominant Western-based precepts of cultural authenticity associating authentic culture with specific belongings and traits, such as a particular language or race (Williams 1993). Indeed, that one's identity is carried in one's blood and thus in one's race has been a primary canon for distinguishing Native Americans in the United States since at least the late 19th century. This is evident in the rise of federal administrative techniques for fixing Indianness around degrees and measurements of blood quantums that in turn are used as the determinant element in apportioning both rights and entitlements to indigenous groups (Biolsi 1995; Turner Strong and Van Winkle 1996). For the Taíno, however, the lack of historical records ascertaining either blood quantums or the veracity of Taíno continuity has rendered Taíno racial features into something to be guarded, promoted, and even policed. The Taíno Inter-Tribal Council of New Jersey, for instance, has even fashioned two membership categories to distinguish applicants of Taíno Native American blood (*Natiao*) from those who lack an indigenous heritage (*Guatiao*)—an assessment mostly made on the basis of an individual's self-identification as such, and the submission of four 1x1 inch color pictures to be reviewed by the Inter-Tribal Membership picture ID review. Applicants whose Taíno Native American blood is verified by their "look," and who state their "willingness to abide by the organizational rules" are then accepted as *Natiao* or "blood brothers," as opposed to *Guatiao*, or "adoptive brothers" (Taíno Inter-Tribal Council 1999).

The result of this concern over the "Taíno look" is the sanctioning of characteristics that favor lighter over darker Taínos. None of the Taínos at the meeting, for instance, excused or rationalized what could be considered their "white" phenotypic characteristics; but some did make a point of asserting their Taínoness "in spite of" their African ancestry. Similarly in Puerto Rico, as I noted elsewhere, the selection of the indigenous queen during the National Indigenous Festival, has traditionally favored "lighter" candidates because the preference for straight hair and copper color discriminate most against black Puerto Ricans, who are identified mostly by their hair and color (Dávila 1997). A candidate with "bad" (tightly curled) hair was therefore far less likely to be selected even if she had other Taíno traits such as high cheekbones, a narrow forehead, and elongated eyes.

Although connected to hierarchies of color and race, the affirmation of Taíno continuity is nonetheless full of implications for the traditional canons of Puerto Rican nationality, and for the historical subversion of alternative conceptions of a Puerto Rican reality. In particular, Taíno assertions that "Puerto Rico is not a homogenous society, that pro-Spanish Puerto Rican groups have falsely misrepresented our national culture" (Guanikeyu Torres on IPR 1997), and criticisms that Puerto Rico's census policies and cultural institutions are "avenues for the colonization of Puerto Ricans into good Spanish European Puerto Ricans" (IPR 1997), do represent undeniable critiques of the historical subversion of issues of difference and race within contemporary discussions of Puerto Rican culture. Again, these claims may be more pressing and poignant on the island than on the mainland, where the recognition of particular ethnic differences has historically served as a key mechanism for politics as well as a tool to organize difference (Cruz 1993; Segal and Handler 1995). In the U.S., appeals to difference are not so much of a challenge to the U.S. nationalist canon or to the discourse of multiculturalism and representation, but an extension of these frameworks that promote specific ends. Nevertheless, in both places, the assertion of Taíno continuity presents a challenge to traditional definitions of Taíno identity, as either subverted or extinct, as well as to who has the right to define its scope and content, be they anthropologists, archaeologists, curators, or representatives of government and cultural institutions.

In particular, in asserting their Taíno identity, these groups find themselves, purposefully or not, confronting colonial frameworks and modes of thinking not only to combat the dominant view of their extinction, but also to attain public recognition of Taíno identity in its own right, rather than on the criteria of anthropologists or scholars. Thus, despite the preference for the so called Taíno look, Taíno activists are simultaneously involved in challenging essentialist constructs of identity that prioritize authenticity and continuity by stressing their identity as one that is fluid and dormant, more cultural than biological, and thus, less based on a proven heritage or on the maintenance of a language, or a defined spirituality or tradition. The reality of hybridity, of mixed and reconstructed traditions looms large in their movement, making the Taíno an identity that is more inclusive than exclusive, and more tolerant than intolerant of the alternative interpretations of Taínoness being concurrently developed by other groups.

It is in this context that memory emerges as an empowering and legitimating element, an expansive realm whereby stories from rural relatives, hunches and premonitions about one's identity, and dreams and prophesies "to follow one's heart" are promoted and validated as "sites of memory" for recovering a long-lost past (Nora 1989). As stated by Naniki Reyes Ocasio, who echoed what was expressed on numerous occasions during the meeting: "They have hidden us from ourselves, but we are lifting our veil. We don't see the '*Americanos*' anymore in the mirror. We are starting to see who we are and that's our dream, to trust our instincts and to not allow anyone to tell us who we are."

Of relevance here is Nora's (1989) distinction between history, as the archival and voluntary representation of selected traditions, and memory as a process of constant evolution by nature, multiple, fluid and spontaneous. Freed from the temporality suggested by Nora's argument, whereby he sees the devouring in modernity of memory by history, this distinction becomes relevant for the understanding of the Taínos' mobilization of memory as a strategy for validating their movement and for escaping traditional modes of authenticating heritage. Again, this issue came to the forefront during the planning meeting at El Museo, when staff members articulated their concerns for distinguishing between "invention" and "continuity" in Taíno traditions and for selecting only validated proofs of Taíno continuity for their exhibit. These concerns were consistently met with indeterminate responses by the contemporary Taínos who challenged such distinctions and emphasized instead the realm of dreams, gestures, and everyday life as the sites of Taíno cultural knowledge. "You would not ask someone to define or give you proof of how to be American or Italian," was one such response that emphasize instead the realm of practice as the latent site for the inscription of memory and thus of continuity with a Taíno past. Being Taíno, they repeatedly argued, was not about certain traits or even about identifying oneself in this manner. Rather, Taíno identity was about a past that is embedded in practices of communality, spirituality, and generosity, pointing to Castells' (1997) observation about the increasing importance of the intangible axioms of "god, nation, family and community" as a recourse for meaning and identity in the global society (1997: 66–67). Accordingly, Taíno identity revolves around ways of being and acting, and the recovering and remembering of values currently under siege, such as spirituality and communality. This makes the Taíno an identity that cannot be "described" as much as lived. Thus, the question to ask people, they argued, was not to define or describe their Taíno identity, but to remember their past and "how things were"—then people's knowledge of the Taíno would come to the forefront.

Of course, I am not suggesting here that these more fluid understandings of identity have freed these groups from conflict over who is more or less Taíno, or about which group is more or less legitimate or authentic. But by challenging public dismissals of their identity, Taínos, if only by sheer need, are simultaneously promoting broader proofs of tradition or continuity. Hence, we have groups such as the Maisiti Yucayeke Taíno, a splinter of the Asociación Indígena Taina in New York, which defines itself as encompassing people irrespective of their religion, sexual orientation, color, language, etc.; while, as evident above, most groups have devised ways of incorporating people committed to furthering Taíno ways and interests as members, supporters, or friends. Similarly, Taíno groups and associations, irrespective of their goals, have tended to conceptualize themselves not so much in nationalist as in diasporic terms. Attempting to recover a population that knew little of geographical boundaries, having spread throughout most of the greater Antilles, most Taíno organizations have tended to reach out beyond national limits to constitute themselves and their membership. Nación Taina for instance, claims to "be not a club or a group or an association or organization, but rather the restoration of an entire people from all over the Caribbean and the U.S. diaspora." To

48

underscore its trans-Caribbean and diasporic identity, Nación Taina has representatives in Cuba, Puerto Rico, and New York (Nación Taina, flyer). The outcome of these trans-Caribbean objectives remains to be ascertained, but we should certainly not ignore their possibilities, considering the historically tense split between populations on the island and the diaspora, and the lack of Caribbean intra-island communication and exchange, itself a product of the islands' colonial and postcolonial history.

In closing, we have many lessons to learn from this movement. Foremost among them is the lack of institutional channels to shape authoritative accounts of history and nationality and to fully eradicate the multiple heterogeneities out of which larger encompassing identities are ultimately forged. Yet another lesson involves the tenacity and resilience of memory, as an active realm in permanent transition, subject to constant reinvention and manipulation. That is, what makes memory a resilient and enduring strategy for contemporary Taínos is precisely its ability to be summoned as an active repository of heritage embodied in everyday life stories, dreams, and gestures—the key to what was dormant but not forgotten. And, indeed the Taíno was never forgotten. The Taíno was always implicated in new myths, uses, and practices. Thus, let us all recall the historical use and manipulation of the Taíno the next time we either scorn or celebrate this movement. If anything, such divergent use brings attention to the inability of reaching a single interpretation, either for the utilization of the Taíno past or for its current revival. Yet looking at the past may very well point us to what may be the cause of discomfort for some and the excitement for others: the sheer realization that the current Taíno revival may affect the Taíno's long-lasting political potential and perhaps its future symbolic malleability. At stake, then, is whether the Taíno, now claimed as a living reality, would continue to serve as a symbol for all Puerto Ricans.

Notes

1. In 1995, for instance, the Consejo General de Taínos Borincanos was invited to participate in the first commemoration of the International Day of the World's Indigenous Peoples by the United Nations.

2. Sued-Badillo's attempt to demystify the legacy of the Taíno is exemplified in his essay of historical rectification entitled "The Caribs, Myth or Reality" (1978). Here, Sued-Badillo argues that the distinction between the Caribs, who are described as a warlike, cannibalistic Caribbean group, and the Taínos, commonly regarded by the chronicles as a peaceful group, was a colonial invention to support the enslavement and exploitation of the indigenous population. In turn, Sued-Badillo's study of the Caribs gives us a perfect example of the politics surrounding the interpretation of Taíno culture because the question of whether the Taínos and Caribs were two distinct cultural groups in the Caribbean has been transformed into a political issue by the advocates of each theory. Sued-Badillo contests the beliefs of Ricardo Alegría, the founder of the Institute of Puerto Rican Culture, that the Taínos and Caribs were in fact two different groups. He considers Alegría "to have manipulated data on the Taínos to fit an ideological portrait of them as ancestral authors of a docility towards invaders that is continued in Puerto Rico's present-day commonwealth arrangement with the United States" (quoted in Stevens-Arroyo 1988: 25).

3. There are indeed Taíno organizations that were founded before the 1990s. Some of the most important U.S. Taíno organizations trace their history to Puerto Rico and claim to have been active since the 1970s. However, it was generally after 1990 and in the mainland United States that the Taíno movement became most established through institutions that either have bylaws, or are incorporated as not-for-profit organizations, and or have attained recognition from wider institutions of society.

4. Planning Session of the Taíno Legacy Project on July 18, 1997, at El Museo del Barrio. This meeting brought together José Barreiro, a member of Taíno Nation and Associate Director of the American Indian Program at Cornell University; Roberto Mucaro Borrero, official representative in the U.S. mainland of the Consejo General de Taínos Borincanos; Jorge Estevez, a Taíno from Quisqueya and a staff member at the National Museum of the American Indian, Smithsonian Institution; Magda Martas, co-Director of Taínos del Norte; Bobby González, co-founder of Taínos del Norte; Naniki Reyes Ocasio, a Taíno tradition-bearer from the island; Miguel Sague, founder of the Kanei Indian Spiritual Circle. The meeting also included museum staff, other Taíno activists; René Moreira, a Garífuna; Peter Ferbel, a U.S.

archaeologist based in the Dominican Republic; and myself. Most of the observations in this work are based on the statements that were made by the Taínos at this meeting dealing with identity and self-identification as a Taíno. There also were subsequent interviews with some of these Taíno groups.

5.   These particular groups also have demanded that they be given official representation with regard to all policies that affect Puerto Ricans, both on the island and the mainland.

6.   These views were also represented in this panel and discussion. See also Dávila (1997).

References

Alegría, Ricardo
   (1974) "La Primera Exposición de Piezas Arqueológicas y el Establecimiento del Primer Museo de Puerto Rico," *Revista del Instituto de Cultura Puertorriqueña*, 64: 37–42.
Biolsi, Thomas
   (1995) "The Birth of the Reservation: Making the Modern Individual Among the Lakota," *American Ethnologist*, 22 (1): 28–54.
Brau, Salvador
   (1978) [1907] *La Colonización de Puerto Rico*. San Juan, Puerto Rico: Instituto de Cultura Puertorriqueña.
Castells, Manuel
   (1997) *The Power of Identity*. New York: Basil Blackwell.
Coll y Toste, Cayetano
   (1968) [1916] "Memoria descriptiva de la primera exposición pública de la industria, agricultura y bellas artes, de la isla de Puerto Rico, en Junio de 1854," in *Boletín Histórico de Puerto Rico,* vol. 3, pp. 173–223. New York: Kraus Reprint Co.
Cruz, Jon
   (1993) "From Farce to Tragedy: Reflections on the Reification of Race at Century's End," in *Mapping Multiculturalism*, Avery Gordon and Christopher Newfield, eds, pp. 19–39. Minneapolis: University of Minnesota Press.
Dávila, Arlene
   (1997) *Sponsored Identities: Cultural Politics in Puerto Rico*. Philadelphia: Temple University Press.
Dimas, Marcos
   (1990) "Taller Alma Boricua: Reflecting on Twenty Years of the Puerto Rican Workshop, 1969–1989," in *Taller Boricua 20th Anniversary Exhibit. El Museo*

del Barrio. September 15–April 15, 1990, pp. 10–15. New York: El Museo del Barrio.

Flores, Juan

(1979) *Insularismo e Ideologia Burguesa.* Havana: Casa de las Americas.

Gelpi, Juan

(1993*)* *Literatura y paternalismo en Puerto Rico.* Rio Piedras, Puerto Rico: Editorial Universidad de Puerto Rico.

Handler, Richard and Jocelyn Linnekin

(1984) "Tradition, Genuine or Spurious," *Journal of American Folklore,* 97 (385): 273–290.

Henige, David

(1991) "On the Contact Population of Hispaniola: History as Higher Mathematics," in *Caribbean Slave Society and Economy,* Hilary Beckels and Verene Shepherd, eds, pp. 2–12. New York: The New Press.

(IPR) Institute for Puerto Rican Policy

(1997) "Show me the Real Puerto Rican Taíno...," *IPR forum,* <ipr@igc.apc.org>

Klor de Alva, Jorge

(1997) "The Invention of Ethnic Origins and the Negotiation of Latino Identity, 1969–1981," in *Challenging Fronteras: Structuring Latina and Latino Lives in the U.S.,* Mary Romero, Pierrette Hondagneu-Sotelo and Vilma Ortiz, eds, pp. 55–74. New York: Routledge.

Knight, Franklin

(1990) *The Caribbean: The Genesis of a Fragmented Nationalism.* New York: Oxford University Press.

Linnekin, Jocelyn

(1991) "Cultural Invention and the Dilemma of Authenticity," *American Anthropologist,* 93 (2): 446–449.

Lipsitz, George

(1991) *Time Passages: Collective Memory and American Popular Culture.* Minneapolis: University of Minnesota Press.

(1997) "Frantic to Join...the Japanese Army: The Asia Pacific War in the Lives of African American Soldiers and Civilians," in *The Politics of Culture in the Shadow of Capital,* Lisa Lowe and David Lloyd, eds, pp. 324–353. Durham: Duke University Press.

Maldonado-Denis, Manuel

(1969) *Puerto Rico: Mito y Realidad.* Barcelona: Ediciones Península.

Moreno, Maria José

(1997) *Identity Formation and Organizational Change in Nonprofit Institutions: A Comparative Study of Two Hispanic Museums.* Ph.D. dissertation. Columbia University.

Nora, Pierre

(1989) "Between Memory and History; Les Lieux de Memoire," *Representations,* 26: 7–25.

Rowe, William and Vivian Schelling
(1991) *Memory and Modernity: Popular Culture in Latin America.* London: Verso.

Segal, Daniel and Richard Handler
(1995) "U.S. Multiculturalism and the Concept of Culture," *Identities: Global Studies in Culture and Power,* 1 (4): 391–408.

Silén, Juan Angel
(1973) *Historia de la Nación Puertorriqueña.* Rio Piedras, Puerto Rico: Editorial Edil.

Stevens-Arroyo, Antonio M.
(1988) *Cave of the Jagua: the mythological world of the Taínos.* Albuquerque: University of New Mexico Press.

Sturken, Marita
(1997) *Tangled Memories: The Vietnam War, The Aids Epidemic, and the Politics of Remembering.* Berkeley: University of California Press.

Sued-Badillo, Jalil
(1978) *Los Caribes: Realidad o Fábula.* Rio Piedras: Editorial Antillana.

Taíno Inter-Tribal Council
(1999) <http://www.hartford-hwp.com/Taíno/index.html>

Turner Strong, Pauline and Barrik Van Winkle
(1996) "Indian Blood: Reflections on the Reckoning and Refiguring of Native North American Identity," *Cultural Anthropology,* 11 (4): 547–576.

Williams, Brackette
(1993) "The Impact of the Precepts of Nationalism on the Concept of Culture: Making Grasshoppers of Naked Apes," *Cultural Critique,* 24: 143–191.

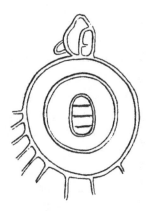

3.

JORGE DUANY

Making Indians Out of Blacks:
The Revitalization of Taíno Identity
in Contemporary Puerto Rico*

If anything characterizes nationalist thought and practice, it is the search for indigenous "roots." Following Benedict Anderson's (1991) renowned definition, nations are typically imagined as communities with a long and illustrious past. In Eric Hobsbawm's (1983) words, nations are "invented traditions" not because they are fictitious (all traditions are actually invented), but because they are fabricated and represented as ancient and sacred essences when they can often be traced to recent and deliberate attempts by intellectuals, politicians, and social movements to create or transform a State. Finally, the quest for native origins is a common discursive practice to "narrate the nation" by including certain "autochthonous" ideological elements and excluding "foreign" ones (Bhabha, ed. 1990).

In colonial societies, the search for indigenous roots acquires a specific symbolism with political repercussions. Perhaps the best-known case is that of pre-1947 India, where nationalist discourse articulated a

*This essay is a revised version of a paper presented at the symposium on "Rethinking Taíno: The Cultural Politics of the Use of their Legacy and Imagery," El Museo del Barrio, New York, February 28, 1998. I would like to thank Arlene Dávila for her kind invitation to write this essay. I also appreciate the comments and suggestions on earlier drafts by Luis Duany, Diana López, and Gabriel Haslip-Viera.

series of moral values, rooted in the native land, history, and religion, against the onslaught of British imperialism (see Chatterjee 1993, 1995; Bhabha 1994; Harassym, 1990). As Partha Chatterjee (1993) has shown, Indian elites developed a patriotic consciousness based on the spiritual regeneration of their native culture. But there are many other cases where cultural nationalism has served to define and crystallize a counter-hegemonic movement against colonial rule. Recent thinking and writing in post-colonial studies have begun to "unpack" the various strategies of resistance, negotiation, and accommodation to British, French, Dutch, U.S., and other imperialisms in Asia, Africa, Latin America, and the Caribbean (see Thomas 1994; Williams and Chrisman 1994; Chambers and Curti 1996). A common gesture of anti-colonial projects everywhere has been to recover, reappraise, and commemorate the "historical patrimony" prior to European and U.S. colonization.

In Puerto Rico, the nativistic movement has historically faced several challenges. First, the Island's original inhabitants were decimated during the first half of the sixteenth century, although their cultural and biological characteristics influenced the development of the local population. Second, Puerto Rico changed colonial masters in 1898, from Spain to the United States, so that nationalists first turned to Spanish, not indigenous culture, as a form of resistance and affirmation against Americanization. Lastly, the massive importation of African slaves throughout most of the Spanish colonial period complicates any search for the pure pre-Columbian or European origins of Puerto Rican culture. When asked to define Cuban—and by extension Caribbean—culture, a Cuban historian recently quipped that all of our ancestors (including those who claim some Taíno heritage) came by boat—whether from Europe, Africa, Asia, or other parts of the Americas.

In this chapter, I propose to interpret the Taíno revival as a symbol of cultural identity in contemporary Puerto Rico. My argument is organized around three working hypotheses. To begin, nationalist intellectuals—particularly anthropologists, archaeologists, and historians—have appropriated and elaborated the Taíno imagery as a central emblem of their nation, literally and metaphorically as "the first root" of Puerto Ricanness. In this effort, scholars have drawn on a long *indigenista* tradition in creative literature, not only in Puerto Rico, but also in the Dominican Republic and

Cuba. A romantic image of the native peoples of the Caribbean has served as the main model for contemporary social scientists.

Furthermore, the Taíno heritage has recently been canonized through state-sponsored institutions such as museums, monuments, festivals, contests, crafts, and textbooks. Unfortunately, much of the re-creation of the indigenous past has entailed the denigration of "the third root," as African culture is commonly called in Puerto Rico. This is what I mean when I use the title phrase, "Making Indians Out of Blacks." It refers to the symbolic displacement of the African by Taíno culture in many scholarly analyses and public representations of Puerto Rican national identity. As in multiethnic and multiracial societies throughout Latin America, nationalist discourse in Puerto Rico has privileged the European and indigenous sources of national identity over the African "other" (see, for example, Wade 1997; Radcliffe and Westwood 1996).

Finally, the growing appeal of cultural—as opposed to political—nationalism on the Island (as well as in the diaspora) is due in large part to the popularity of Taíno iconography, alongside the central Hispanic component. Cultural nationalism should not be seen as a lesser or minor form of political nationalism, as the pejorative labels "neo-nationalism" and "lite nationalism" seem to imply. Cultural nationalism represents a serious attempt to assert Puerto Rico's distinctive collective identity, within the context of continued political and economic dependence on the United States. Like Arlene Dávila (1997: 3), I will approach cultural nationalism "not as an apolitical development but as part of a shift in the terrain of political action to the realm of culture and cultural politics, where the idiom of culture constitutes a dominant discourse to advance, debate, and legitimize conflicting claims." Unlike Dávila, I would argue that this turn to culture has a strong potential to ideologically subvert the colonial regime in Puerto Rico. Toward the end of this essay, I will return to the thorny question of the repercussions of cultural nationalism for the anticolonial struggle on the Island.

Intellectual Discourses on the Taíno Indians

The scholarly revitalization of the Taíno Indians in Puerto Rico has undergone five distinct moments or phases. The first serious efforts to study the pre-Columbian peoples of the Island began in the mid-nineteenth century, under the influence of the Romantic movement, closely linked with the *indigenista* and *costumbrista* schools of literature (Alegría 1978; López de Molina 1980). Since 1847, Puerto Rican writers had cultivated the Indian theme as part of their patriotic exaltation of the New World natives vis-à-vis the Spanish conquistadors (Corchado Juarbe 1993). Much of the renewed interest in the Taíno Indians was fueled by the efforts of Creole elites to distinguish themselves from *peninsulares*. As in the rest of Latin America, "Creole" in Puerto Rico came to be identified with everything native, local, or typical of the land and people of the Americas.

The founders of Puerto Rican prehistory were actually trained in other fields of study, such as zoologist Agustín Stahl, historians Cayetano Coll y Toste and Salvador Brau, and literary critic and poet Luis Lloréns Torres. Leading amateurs, private collectors, and dilettantes included George Latimer, José Julián Acosta, and Father José María Nazario. This early stage in the reconstruction of the Taíno heritage was marked by debates regarding the proper place of the indigenous cultures of the Caribbean in a larger evolutionary scale; the ideological influence of biological and geographic determinism; and the growing recognition of "the remarkable beauty and finish of the stone implements of Porto Rico [sic] and others of the Antilles," as one American writer employed by the Smithsonian Institution put it (Mason 1877: 372). The romantic "rediscovery" of the indigenous roots of Puerto Rican culture might be an apt term to summarize this first trend.

A second moment in the development of the Taíno heritage as cultural capital on the Island involved the gradual accumulation of highly technical data on the pre-Columbian peoples of the Caribbean. This stage was characterized by the growing professionalization of archaeological research on the subject. Roughly between 1898 and 1945, most archaeologists (primarily from the United States) focused on the detailed historical reconstruction of the Taíno Indians and their predecessors (see Rouse 1992 and

Duany 1987 for summaries of this research). By the 1930s, the dominant paradigm in anthropology worldwide had shifted from evolutionism to historical particularism and especially to diffusionism. Stripped from the bluntest forms of racial thinking, scholars pursued their interests in Taíno art and mythology and explored the cultural contacts between the circum-Caribbean and Mesoamerica in prehistoric times.

Pablo Morales Cabrera (1932), a self-proclaimed aficionado, and Adolfo de Hostos (1941), then official historian of Puerto Rico, wrote extensively on the traditional beliefs and customs of the Island's aborigines. Both essays, each in its own way, offer glimpses into the state of knowledge on the Taíno Indians during the first half of the twentieth century. Both display a fascination with indigenous art, particularly sculptures made of stone, clay, wood, and bone. This aesthetic appreciation is a recurrent theme in the contemporary use and elaboration of visual images from the pre-Columbian past.

The third moment in the Taíno revival began shortly after World War II and extends into the present. A nationalist "reappropriation" of the indigenous legacy captures the essence of this phase. In 1947, Ricardo Alegría founded the Center for Archaeological Research and directed the Museum of History, Anthropology, and Art at the University of Puerto Rico in Río Piedras. Although Alegría (1957) conducted pioneering ethnographic fieldwork on the descendants of African slaves, he specialized mostly in archaeological research on the pre-Columbian populations of Puerto Rico. Alegría, Eugenio Fernández Méndez, and other Puerto Rican scholars were apparently inspired by nationalist concepts of cultural identity based on *indigenismo* and *mestizaje,* such as those developed in Mexico during the 1920s and 1930s by Manuel Gamio and José Vasconcelos (see Martínez-Echazábal 1998).

The definitive statement on the Taíno Indians from a cultural nationalist perspective is precisely Alegría's *Historia de nuestros indios (versión elemental)* (1950). This short text clearly reveals the deployment of "our Indians" as one of the historical foundations of contemporary Puerto Rican identity. Here Alegría synthesizes the available archaeological and historical evidence to provide a sympathetic account of indigenous values and practices. His portrait highlights the Taínos' happiness, simplicity, tranquility, peacefulness, and innocence prior to the arrival of Columbus.

The graphic illustrations by his wife, Carmen Pons de Alegría, represent everyday scenes from the Indians' lifestyle, from sleeping in hammocks and rowing in canoes to playing in their ball courts and dancing their ritual *areítos*. This essay and its accompanying images have become one of the most widely disseminated texts of *indigenista* discourse on the Island.

Another key work of the cultural nationalist project dominant during this period is Eugenio Fernández Méndez's *Art and Mythology of the Taíno Indians of the Greater West Indies* (1972). Fernández Méndez was the first professor of anthropology at the University of Puerto Rico as well as the first president of the board of directors of the Institute of Puerto Rican Culture in 1955. Although more specialized than Alegría's "elementary version," *Art and Mythology* depicts the Taínos in a similar light. The author argues that the original inhabitants of Puerto Rico had developed a distinctive artistic style prior to the Spanish Conquest. He focuses on the Taínos' religious icons—the *cemíes*—to reconstruct their world view and shows that they had a relatively advanced aesthetic sense of life, similar to that of the Maya. Along with Alegría, Fernández Méndez contributed to the consolidation of Taíno imagery as a sign of the Island's national culture.

Although the latter trend continues today, the fourth stage in the intellectual discourse on the Taíno Indians (initiated during the mid-1970s) was the criticism of established knowledge. "Rebuttal" of past claims might be an appropriate label for this approach to the indigenous legacy. Contemporary archaeologists and historians such as Diana López Sotomayor (1975), Jalil Sued Badillo (1978, 1995b), Miguel Rodríguez (1984), and Francisco Moscoso (1986) have distanced themselves from the official treatment of the "first root." A good example of this trend is Sued Badillo's (1978) work on the Carib Indians, which he claims were a fable invented by Spanish conquistadors to justify warfare and enslavement (see also Sued Badillo 1995a). Rather than romantically search for the "lost link" of Puerto Rican culture, many scholars are now engaged in the painstaking documentation and reassessment of the pre-Columbian past, often employing insights from historical materialism.

Although current archaeological studies are still commonly framed in terms of the need to preserve the Island's national patrimony, they tend to concentrate on highly specialized issues with little practical relevance for

60

cultural nationalism (see, for example, Chanlatte Baik 1976, 1986, 1990; Instituto de Cultura Puertorriqueña 1997). Now that the indigenous heritage has become a public asset, so to speak, many scholars have retreated into an academic posture that tends to take for granted the dominant representation of the Taíno Indians as an emblem of Puerto Rican identity. Since the 1980s, archaeological research on the pre-Columbian populations of the Island has been stimulated by federal legislation mandating excavations prior to developing real estate, locally known as *arqueología de contrato* (see Asociación Puertorriqueña de Antropólogos y Arqueólogos 1990). With the upsurge in "contract archaeology," the idea of "rescuing" the Taíno heritage has receded somewhat in importance, and the concept of "cultural resource management" has gained wider currency. This label might be used to characterize the fifth and most recent phase in the study of the indigenous populations of Puerto Rico.

The current "culture wars" at the Institute of Puerto Rican Culture, especially as a result of recent administrative and policy shifts, have softened the nationalist rhetoric of "rescue archaeology." Note the subdued tone of the following introduction to a recent collection of archaeological essays: "The dissemination of the nature and value of our archaeological patrimony holds great importance for the development of the study of our history and the enrichment of our artistic-cultural heritage" (Instituto de Cultura Puertorriqueña 1997: i; my translations throughout). The adjective "national" seems to have disappeared from the author's vocabulary. It is no coincidence that the Partido Nuevo Progresista, which favors statehood for the Island, has controlled the Commonwealth government—including the Institute of Puerto Rican Culture—since 1992. Thus, the appropriation of the Indian theme by state authorities has become a contested terrain between cultural nationalists and annexationists. The issue is part of a wider struggle to define the nation from various ideological perspectives (see Flores Collazo 1998).

Lessons from the Indigenous Past

This brief "genealogy" of Taíno studies on the Island suggests several patterns. First, the virtual extinction of the native people of Puerto Rico during the Spanish colonial period has forced scholars to rely primarily on incomplete archaeological and historical sources of information, and secondarily on cross-cultural and linguistic evidence, such as related ethnographic research on Amazonia (López-Baralt 1985). Large gaps in anthropological knowledge have often been filled with wild speculation, fantasy, and myth. The virtual absence of prehistoric monuments—comparable to the Maya pyramids of Chichen Itzá or the Inca city of Machu Pichu—has led cultural nationalists to look elsewhere in their reconstruction of the indigenous past in Puerto Rico. At the same time, the scarcity of ethnohistorical data has proved convenient for those engaged in the invention of tradition.

From the beginning, the most useful remains of Taíno material culture were their abundant and prodigious ceramics, including a large number and variety of pottery, beads, amulets, collars, masks, and stools. Archaeological collections of these artifacts were repeatedly canvassed to show that the Taínos were not savages (Mason 1877: 391); that they had attained a higher stage of culture than the Caribs or the Ciboneys (Coll y Toste 1979 [1897]); and that they were actually "quite developed" in their socioeconomic integration and religious beliefs (Fernández Méndez 1972: 43). The survival of Taíno art thus encouraged their retrieval as a relatively advanced indigenous people prior to their European "discovery." This was a necessary step in their retrospective reassessment for contemporary nationalistic purposes.

A common thread in the Taíno revival has been the romantic impulse. The standard treatment of the Indians as a symbol of Puerto Rican identity (as opposed to Spanish) first emerged in creative literature—especially in poetry—toward the end of the nineteenth century through such major figures as Eugenio María de Hostos. In the twentieth century, leading writers like Enrique Laguerre, Juan Antonio Corretjer, and René Marqués have employed the Taíno figure as an inspiration in the unfinished quest for the Island's freedom, now from the United States (Corchado Juarbe 1993; Ayala-Richards 1995). Although not all scholars succumbed to the temptation of idealizing the indigenous heritage, most converged with the nationalist canon in literature and politics.

Stahl initiated a long tradition in the recovery of the Taínos when he wrote: "I propose in this work to awaken their image *[despertar su recuerdo]* in the memory of men of learning and of the *borincanos* who have replaced them" (1897: v). Moreover, Stahl's exalted rhetorical tone is typical of *indigenista* writing of his period: "that desire [to know the Indians]... sprouts spontaneously from the soul that loves the memories of this land where one's eyes first saw the brilliant light of the tropical sun, where one's cradle once rocked and the happy days of one's pleasant youth drifted, and where one's ashes will probably rest" (p. 3). Lloréns Torres's (1967 [1898]: 84–85) classic statement is also worth quoting here at length:

> *without any kind of commodities and means to develop their well-being, as befitted their semi-savage life, [the Taíno Indians] passed the happy days of their existence, without hate or rancor, without internal struggles, and enjoying the delights of the agreeable paradise under whose leafy trees another people will not drift as united by fortune, by happiness, by affection, and by the most fervent love that their small fatherland inspired in them.*

Most nationalist intellectuals since then have shared Stahl's and Lloréns Torres's enthusiasm for the Taínos, from Adolfo de Hostos's re-evaluation of Taíno art for its "pristine innocence" (1941: 89), to Fernández Méndez's characterization of Taíno ceramics as "superior" to all the ceramics of northern South America (1972: 72). Furthermore, scholars have tended to claim the Indians as "ours," while paying lip service to their regional distribution throughout the Greater Antilles. Even today, detailed maps of the Caribbean are notably scarce in archaeological museums in Puerto Rico. Finally, the nativistic movement has focused specifically on the Taíno heritage, rather than on the full range of pre-Columbian cultures, including the igneri or the so-called archaic peoples of the Island.

A recurrent theme in the *indigenista* literature over the past century has been the glowing portrayal of the Taíno "character." From Stahl to Alegría, the pre-Columbian inhabitants of Borinquen have been typified as "sweet, affable, serviceable, peaceful, and hospitable" (Stahl 1889: 119), terms that keep appearing in contemporary descriptions of Puerto Ricans.

In contrast to the Caribs, usually depicted as "warlike and adventure-some, blood-thirsty and cruel cannibals" (Coll y Toste 1979 [1897]: 57), the Taínos become the prototype of Rousseau's "noble savage." The constant reiteration of the same adjectives—docile, sedentary, indolent, tranquil, chaste—from one author to another acquires ritual and mythical connotations. Such traits have even become basic elements in standard notions of Puerto Rico's "national character" (see, for instance, Marqués 1977).

Since the end of the nineteenth century, Puerto Rican scholars have represented the Taíno as an essentially good figure, with a peaceful and generous nature, a relatively simple but respectable way of life, and a spiritual innocence uncontaminated by Western civilization. The Island's environment itself—Lloréns Torres's "agreeable paradise"—has typically been depicted as fertile, abundant, placid, and benevolent to human settlement, if not especially conducive to intellectual or moral progress. This Eden-like characterization of indigenous culture and nature has had enormous ideological value for writers engaged in the construction of a national identity on the Island, especially in the second half of the twentieth century. Nothing can be more useful for nationalists than the founding myth of a land and people spoiled by foreign invasion. As Sued Badillo (1995b: 27) points out, "This [national] consciousness expresses that the reality of Puerto Rico is rooted in its mythical geography, a sacred past that is Amerindian in origin and meaning and geographic in its present attributes."

Another discursive practice of Puerto Rican intellectuals has been to overstress the physical traits of the Taíno Indians, primarily to distinguish them from (but also to blur the differences with) those of black slaves. For instance, Brau (1972 [1894]) was at pains to clarify the original meaning of the folk term *cobrizo* (copper-like or tanned) as opposed to *moreno* (literally wheat-colored, or dark-skinned, a euphemism for black in Puerto Rico), when applied to the Taíno phenotype. More recently, the literary critic María Teresa Babín (1986: 48) noted: "In the physical type of numerous 'Indian-looking' Puerto Ricans *(aindiados)* there sometimes seem to reincarnate the beautiful and straight black hair, the pale and lusterless *(mate)* skin, and the slanted eyes with an unfathomable gaze that form our ancestral memory of the physical traits of the *borincano* Indian." Note the rhetorical whitening of the indigenous population in both passages, as well as its romanticization in the second quote.

Until the mid-twentieth century, anthropological thought usually characterized the Taínos as an "inferior race," compared to Europeans, but superior to Africans. Stahl, Brau, Coll y Toste, and Lloréns Torres all shared the viewpoint that the Indians' "racial" characteristics made them physically and intellectually subordinate to the "brave," "indomitable," and "imperturbable" Spaniards (Brau 1972 [1894]: 82). But they also shared the conviction that Africans (or Ethiopians, as they were often called then) were even more "primitive" and "savage" than the Taínos. A similar belief ranked the Taínos higher than the Caribs in their evolutionary scheme.

Although later authors avoid such blatantly ethnocentric and racist terms, many still imply that the Indians were neither white nor black, but brown or "copper-like," and their intermediate phenotype placed them in between European and Africans in ethnic, moral, and aesthetic terms. Few standard descriptions of the Taíno Indians fail to mention their skin color, physical stature, bodily constitution, hair texture, or facial features (see, for example, Alegría 1950). The current social studies curriculum from elementary school to the college level highlights such physical features as "essential" to an understanding of Puerto Ricanness, as any nine-year old child on the Island can easily recite them. For example, a third-grade textbook widely used in Puerto Rico today (Vizcarrondo 1994: 57) lists the following "characteristic traits of the Taíno race:" medium height, copper-tone skin, black and straight hair, prominent cheekbones, slightly slanted eyes, long nose, and relatively thick lips. These features are sharply contrasted with the phenotypes of both Spaniards and Africans.

The idea that "the indigenous element is alive and persists" (Babín 1986: 48) in the racial makeup of contemporary Puerto Rico has gained wide currency. A pseudoscientific study of University of Puerto Rico students even went so far as to classify one fifth of its sample as "Indianic" *(indiado)*, ten times as many blacks (Rodríguez Olleros 1974). In a promotional brochure for the Museo del Indio in Old San Juan, Alegría recently underlined "the typically Indian physical traits that characterize Puerto Ricans: copper-colored skin, straight hair and prominent cheekbones, among others" (Alegría, n.d.). The above-cited textbook asks students to think about people they have met in Puerto Rico with "the same or similar physical traits to those of the Taínos," as well as Spaniards, but not Africans (Vizcarrondo 1994: 57).

The racialization of the Taíno is a key to the symbolic displacement from the African to the indigenous sources of Puerto Rican culture, common in much nationalist discourse on the Island. By pitting the two "races" against each other, nationalist intellectuals have traditionally blended the physical and cultural traits of Taínos and Africans. Historically, this strategy resulted in the overextension of the folk term *indio*, rather than *negro* or *mulato,* to refer to dark-skinned people throughout the Hispanic Caribbean (Roberts 1997). For instance, the Dominican government officially classifies most of its citizens into one of two categories—*indio claro* or *indio oscuro*—but reserves *negro* for the much-despised Haitians. The semantic equation between "Indian" and "black" has served to camouflage the African origins of a large share of the Cuban, Dominican, and Puerto Rican populations.

More recently, the confusion between Indians and blacks has produced endless debates about the "real" origins of musical instruments, culinary traditions, linguistic expressions, and other cultural practices. An academic example of this trend is Babín's *La cultura de Puerto Rico* (1986), which easily attributes an exclusive indigenous origin to such Creole foods as *alcapurrias, mofongo,* and *pasteles,* which probably have some African influence as well (see Alvarez Nazario 1974). On a popular level, a local television commercial for a food distributing company during the 1980s represented three moments in the development of Puerto Rican cuisine: indigenous, Spanish, and modern (i.e., American), but not African. Such discursive practices literally render blacks invisible.

In their effort to "rescue" the Taíno heritage, Puerto Rican scholars have tended to downplay the African contribution to their culture. This gesture is evident in Manuel Alvarez Nazario's (1992) monumental work on the history of the Spanish language in Puerto Rico, which argues that the Taínos contributed many more words than any African language to the local dialect. Unfortunately, the largely positive attempt to recover the "first root" is often predicated on a denial of the "third root" of Puerto Rican culture. As Dávila (1994) has argued, the symbolic elaboration of the Indian has all too often been a way of dismissing the Island's African legacy. The natives' relatively light skin color, plus their physical disappearance as a people and the dearth of reliable information on many crucial aspects of their culture, has helped to mythicize them and overstate their current impact, usually at the expense of blacks.

Institutionalizing the Taíno Heritage

By the mid-1970s, when the anthropologist Ronald Duncan (1978) surveyed college students in San Germán, the Taíno revival had reached canonical status in Puerto Rico. Most of those interviewed believed that the Indians constituted one of the historical "roots" of contemporary Puerto Rican culture. Although many respondents could not specify what beliefs and customs had an indigenous origin, most could mention a few Taíno words and other tokens of their material culture, such as the *cemíes* (the small stone idols) or the *bateyes* (the ceremonial ball courts). Duncan concluded that the Taínos had become an important icon of Puerto Rican identity, despite incomplete archaeological and historical knowledge. Between World War II and the 1970s, the pre-Columbian Indian legacy was consolidated as a cornerstone of national culture. How did this indigenous emblem transcend the narrow confines of an intellectual elite in a colonial society?

The answer to this question lies in the recent political and cultural history of the Island, especially since the creation of the Estado Libre Asociado in 1952, the constitutional formula for limited self-government under colonial rule by the United States. The meteoric rise to power of the Partido Popular Democrático between 1940 and 1968 meant, among other things, the ideological displacement of political nationalism by a new autonomist project with a strong populist orientation, emphasizing economic development through industrialization while preserving close political ties with the United States (Alvarez-Curbelo and Rodríguez Castro 1993). This project also entailed the selective appropriation of nationalist symbols and practices (such as the national flag and anthem) through what came to be known as "Operation Serenity." Former Governor Luis Muñoz Marín (1985 [1953]) himself noted the need to assert and preserve

Puerto Rico's own "personality" in the midst of sweeping socioecono-mic changes. Cultural nationalism became increasingly strong on the Island after the establishment of the Instituto de Cultura Puertorriqueña in 1955 (see Alegría 1978; Aguiló Ramos 1987; Dávila 1997; Flores Collazo 1998).

The Institute's founder and director for 18 years, Ricardo Alegría, was the author of the canonical text on the Taíno Indians in Puerto Rico. He also developed and applied the most influential model of national culture on the Island to date: the notion that Puerto Rican culture was the result of the harmonious integration of three roots—the Indian, Spanish, and African (Ramírez 1985; Aguiló Ramos 1987). Under Alegría's leadership, the Institute initiated "a systematic rediscovery of our cultural patrimony," including the indigenous peoples of the Island (Alegría 1978: 382). A com-prehensive series of lectures, conferences, documentaries, exhibits, recitals, publications, courses, seminars, and research projects was sponsored with local government funds. Perhaps the most relevant initiative was the acqui-sition and development of archaeological collections on the aboriginal population of Puerto Rico.

By the early 1970s, the Institute had established a major museum devoted exclusively to the Indians in Utuado (Centro Ceremonial Cagua-na) and a smaller one in San Juan (Museo del Indio). In addition, Alegría proposed the creation of a Museum of Aboriginal Cultures to house a growing number of pre-Columbian clay and stone pieces owned by the Institute. All of these institution-building efforts were part of a larger agenda of "providing Puerto Rico with new museums where our compa-triots can rediscover their history and culture and feel proud of their nationality" (Alegría 1971: 1). Commemorating and displaying the nation in public places became one of the Institute's main activities. In practice, most of the museums focused on the Spanish colonial heritage, especially the military and religious architecture and art of the nineteenth century, particularly in Old San Juan (although smaller museums throughout the Island did not specialize as much on Hispanic traditions as on local his-tory and culture). The Taíno legacy played a secondary but important role in the public representation of Puerto Ricanness through museums, text-books, and other cultural activities such as festivals and crafts.

Before 1955, the Island had only one museum: the University of

Puerto Rico's Museum of History, Anthropology, and Art, located at the Río Piedras campus. Founded in 1951, the Museum later moved to its present building designed by the architect Henry Clumb at the entrance to the campus. Today, the Museum is divided into three main sections: the Egyptian hall, archaeology hall, and Francisco Oller hall. The archaeology hall houses one of the most extensive selections of Taíno and pre-Taíno artifacts in the Caribbean, including the collections of Adolfo de Hostos and Montalvo Guenard. The Center for Archaeological Research, long devoted to the study of the native peoples of the region, is affiliated with the Museum. Beyond the accidental reasons for the acquisition and development of its three disparate collections (ancient, "primitive," and Impressionist art), their inclusion in the same space tends to equate Taíno culture with Egyptian and French cultures. Thus, Puerto Rican visitors to the Museum can feel justifiably proud of their ancestral roots, as much as they may be impressed by Oller's monumental painting, *El velorio*, or the mummy of a long dead Egyptian queen.

Over the past four decades, the Institute of Puerto Rican Culture has developed an extensive network of museums and parks throughout the Island. At this writing, the Institute administers 13 museums and is restoring seven additional ones. Of these, three are devoted to the indigenous theme: the Museo del Indio and the Museo Puertorriqueño in San Juan, and the Centro Ceremonial Indígena near Utuado. The Museo del Indio documents the indigenous cultures of Puerto Rico from their arrival to the Island thousands of years ago through their disappearance during the Spanish colonial period. The Museo Puertorriqueño was projected to provide a panoramic view of the Island's culture but recently merged with the Institute's Indian collection because of a shortage of funds and administrative restructuring.

The Caguana Ceremonial Center is considered the most important of its kind in the Antilles because of its 11 large ball courts *(bateyes)* lined with ancient monoliths. The Institute has also preserved the adjacent area as a botanical garden that recreates the plants used for food and building materials by the indigenous peoples of Puerto Rico. Thus, visitors to the site make a strong visual connection between the native soil and the aboriginal population. This is undoubtedly the centerpiece of the Institute's *indigenista* project. An official promotional brochure holds that here "the collective soul of Puerto Rican Indians expressed itself through sports and religious rituals." Note the spiritual emphasis of this quote as well as the attempt to commemorate a sacred landscape for the origins of contemporary "Puerto Rican" culture.

In addition to the Institute's museums throughout the Island, two important exhibits of Taíno art are located in Ponce and San Juan (smaller collections have been founded at the Catholic University in Ponce and Turabo University in Caguas). After Caguana, Tibes is the second most important indigenous ceremonial center of the Caribbean, according to a semiofficial promotion (L. Rodríguez 1998). The archaeological site was accidentally discovered in 1975 by a local resident and was later studied and preserved by a regional group of archaeologists, historians, engineers, and geologists called Sociedad Guaynía. Although considered part of the "national patrimony," the Tibes Ceremonial Center was acquired by the Ponce Municipal Government. Tibes provides a forceful example of how the nationalist discourse is played out in a regional context.

Local authorities administer the museum, exhibit hall, and surrounding landscape, but their overall design and function are very similar to the Institute's structures. For instance, the entrance to the archaeological site holds a botanical garden with indigenous plants reminiscent of those found at Caguana. At Tibes as well as elsewhere, tour guides make an explicit connection between "our Indians" and "our indigenous plants." A small Indian village *(yucayeque)* has been constructed in both Tibes and Caguana to recreate the sites' original atmosphere. At Tibes, employees frequently dress themselves in Indian garb to re-enact the Taínos' everyday life, complete with their own version of the native ball game. School teachers throughout the Island encourage their students to draw, paint, carve, and write about the pre-Columbian past to commemorate the Spanish "Discovery" of Puerto Rico. Their work is then showcased in the Tibes museum and exhibit hall.

The institutionalization of Taíno imagery has gone hand in hand with its growing commercialization. Over the last few decades, indigenous motifs have become increasingly fashionable in Puerto Rico—from naming practices to T-shirts and tourist merchandise. Every year, the town of Jayuya celebrates a "national indigenous festival" in which a "Taíno-looking" woman is crowned queen (Dávila 1997). Folk dance groups constantly dramatize native *areítos* for foreign as well as local consumption. Artisans and engravers have incorporated Taíno motifs in their crafts, posters, and murals. Since the 1970s, transnational corporations such as those that manufacture Mazola cooking oil and Winston cigarettes have featured indigenous references in their advertising campaigns. A local insurance agency, GA Life, recently issued a photographic calendar on the Taíno heritage. Puerto Rico's official tourist magazine, *Qué Pasa,* usually showcases the indigenous heritage—especially in arts and crafts—but underplays African culture as an integral part of the Island's history. Native folklore, especially the omnipresent *cemí,* has become a marketable commodity in Puerto Rico.

The Cultural Politics of Taíno Symbolism

It seems, then, that the intellectual discourse on national identity, with its strong emphasis on the recovery of the Island's indigenous roots, has been popularized to a significant degree in contemporary Puerto Rico. On the one hand, this trend may be read as a positive and necessary step in the construction of an imagined community, to cite again Anderson's definition of the nation. Growing awareness of their pre-Columbian heritage has provided Puerto Ricans with a longer and more complete view of their past, apart from their colonial histories under Spain and the United States. The widespread cult of the "first root" has instilled local pride and collective identification, which have helped to defend, promote, and even invent new traditions. The mythical image of Borinquen as a tropical paradise uncorrupted by Western civilization has sustained several generations of Puerto Ricans on the Island and in the diaspora. The surge of various grassroots movements in the United States and Puerto Rico claiming descent from the "Taíno nation" is a recent case in point.

On the other hand, the *indigenista* discourse has contributed to the erasure of the ethnic and cultural presence of blacks in Puerto Rico. In the past, anthropologists, archaeologists, and historians explicitly compared Taínos and Africans, invariably concluding that the Indians were physically more attractive, intellectually more capable, and culturally more developed than blacks. While the Taínos were vindicated as noble savages,

71

blacks were despised as primitive others, along with Carib Indians. Evolutionary thinking typically relegated African peoples to the lowest ranks of cultural development on a global scale. Racialized images of Indians and blacks have dominated the way Puerto Ricans imagined their ethnic background.

Although most contemporary scholars have abandoned such racial doctrines, they continue to overrate the pre-Columbian past while downgrading the African contribution to Puerto Rican culture, thus "making Indians out of blacks." As I have argued before, such discursive practices have their institutional impact on lived experiences. A proposal by Alegría (1971) to create a Museum on the Legacy of African Cultures over two decades ago was never supported by the government. A current inventory of museums and monuments mentions no historical sites commemorating the black presence on the Island, while indigenous objects are widely displayed in Barranquitas, Caguas, Coamo, Jayuya, Ponce, San Juan, Utuado, Vieques, and Yabucoa (Departamento de Educación 1992). The only major exhibit on "the third root," co-sponsored by the Institute of Puerto Rican Culture, was quickly dismantled after the Quincentennial Commemoration of the Discovery of Puerto Rico in 1993 (see González 1993).

Under Alegría's direction, the Institute of Puerto Rican Culture defined the broad contours of the dominant culturalist project of the Estado Libre Asociado. Like Fernández Méndez (1980) and other local intellectuals, Alegría believed that Puerto Rico could maintain its own national culture while remaining politically and economically tied to the United States. Both anthropologists defined culture as a spiritual configuration of moral values compatible with an autonomous government. As Fernández Méndez (1980: 42) wrote, "a nationality can exist without the political organization of the sovereign State." Alegría's (1996: 11) view of national culture closely paralleled Fernández Méndez's idealistic approach: for him, "Culture is, above all, a concept and a way of life; it is a spiritual state that defines the physiognomy of a people, of a nationality."

Cultural nationalism became state policy through the Institute of Puerto Rican Culture. The Institute enshrined the organic metaphor of the "three roots:"

> *From the beginning we defined national culture as the prod-*
> *uct of the integration that in the course of four centuries*
> *and a half had taken place in Puerto Rico among the*
> *respective cultures of the Taíno Indians that inhabited the*
> *Island at the time of the Discovery, of the Spaniards who*
> *conquered and colonized it, and of the black Africans who*
> *since the first decades of the sixteenth century began to be*
> *incorporated into our population. (Alegría 1996: 9; see also*
> *Babín 1986: 36)*

This long quote from Alegría reveals the chronological and ideological ranking of the three main ethnic groups on the Island—first Indians, then Spaniards, finally Africans. It also suggests how cultural nationalists have represented each of these groups: the Taínos as the Island's original inhabitants, the Spaniards as conquerors and colonizers, and Africans as late arrivals to be incorporated into "our" culture. Note also that the only racially marked group in this passage are the "black" Africans, not Indians or Spaniards, who thereby appear colorless or equally light-skinned.

This ethnic/racial hierarchy is graphically encoded in the official seal of the Institute of Puerto Rican Culture. The seal represents a well-dressed Spaniard in the center with a book in his hand and three Catholic crosses in the background; to his right stands a semi-nude Taíno with a *cemi* and a corn plant; to his left, a topless African holds a machete, with a *vejigante* mask laying at his feet and a sugar cane plant on one side. This visual representation has multiple symbolic connotations, among them the suggestion that the main contribution of African slaves in Puerto Rico was less cultural than economic, that is, their labor power as cane cutters. The image also suggests that Catholicism was one of the foundations of Puerto Rican culture, represented by the lamb directly underneath the Spanish figure. In principle, the three figures are on an equal footing, thus evoking the myth of peaceful coexistence among separate races and cultures (see Buitrago Ortiz 1982).

In practice, the Institute has assigned different priorities to each of the three "roots." Most of the Institute's programs have focused on the preservation, restoration, and promotion of the Island's Hispanic heritage, particularly in architecture, history, painting, popular arts, folk music, theater, and poetry. Perhaps their most notable achievement has been the conservation and recuperation of the colonial district of Old San Juan as part of the Island's national patrimony. The Institute has also sponsored historical, archaeological, and folklore research and publications. Furthermore, it has spearheaded the commemoration of historical figures (*hombres ilustres*)—mostly upper-class white males—as well as naming public places in their honor. As a result of its numerous initiatives, Alegría claims (1996) that the Institute has fostered a growing national pride among elite as well as popular sectors.

A secondary focus of the Institute has been the study, collection, and display of pre-Columbian artifacts. Rediscovering and exhibiting the indigenous roots of Puerto Rican culture became an important item on the Institute's research agenda, museum-building efforts, and educational projects. The Institute acquired a valuable archaeological collection, second only to the University of Puerto Rico's Museum of History, Anthropology, and Art. Indigenous designs such as the now famous petroglyphs were actively promoted through the Institute's graphic arts program. An entire folk arts industry producing beads, shells, and bracelets has developed around Taíno icons as widely recognized symbols of national identity. These cultural objects are marketed by a well-organized system involving state officials in San Juan, regional centers throughout the Island, and local communities and artisans (Dávila 1997).

Unfortunately, the "third root" of Puerto Rican culture has not received as much official attention as the first two roots, the Taíno and the Spanish. As mentioned before, the lack of a permanent space to document the cultural legacy of black Africans and their descendants contrasts sharply with the proliferation of museums and parks consecrated to Spanish and Taíno traditions in Puerto Rico. Compared to over a dozen museums showcasing Spanish and indigenous traditions, not a single one focuses on the African element. (At the time of this writing, an itinerant exhibition on African art, organized with the New York International African Institute, could be seen at the University of Puerto Rico's Museum. However, the "foreign" and temporary nature of this display suggests that Africans are still represented as external to Puerto Rican culture.) A promising development has been the emergence of a grassroots

74

movement to establish a Museum on the African Man and Woman in Humacao. Only recently has a growing group of scholars begun to question the established "conspiracy of silence" surrounding the persistence of racial prejudice and discrimination on the Island (Routté-Gómez 1995).

Conclusion

In keeping with the official discourse on national identity, Puerto Rican museums have represented the Island's historical patrimony primarily as the Spanish colonial heritage and secondarily as the pre-Columbian indigenous tradition. Nationalist intellectuals have constructed and elaborated a coherent but incomplete image of the Island's cultural identity based on a selective reading of its history, which tends to exclude the African component and celebrate the Indian heritage. From a conventional nationalist standpoint, the political value of recovering the black legacy seems minor compared to the need to establish the ideological link between the pre-Columbian past and the present. The black "root" has been systematically "uprooted" from the main "trunk" of the Puerto Rican nation.

Since the 1950s, the telluric metaphor of the "three roots" has organized much of the dominant representation of Puerto Rican culture, thanks largely to the work of Ricardo Alegría and other intellectuals and artists working with the Institute of Puerto Rican Culture. Alegría's vision of the historical patrimony as constituted primarily by the defense of the Spanish vernacular, the commemoration of national heroes and foundational events, and the development of the arts in their elite and popular manifestations has permeated standard views of Puerto Ricanness in the second half of the twentieth century (see Aguiló Ramos 1987). Recent studies have confirmed the strong ideological consensus on these core symbols across political parties and social classes (Morris 1995; Rivera 1996). Alegría's own archaeological and historical research into the Taíno heritage illustrates the use of the Island's native roots to strengthen the sense of continuity between the Hispanic heritage and the pre-Columbian past. Following a long-standing literary tradition in the Spanish Antilles, nationalists have called upon the Taíno Indians as a symbolic resource to reaffirm patriotic values in Puerto Rico (see Ayala-Richards 1995). After World War II, the local intellectual elite was able to consolidate its culturalist project of the nation without creating a State.

The official adoption of cultural nationalism by the Commonwealth government has had mixed results. On the positive side, the Institute of Puerto Rican Culture and other cultural institutions such as the Ateneo Puertorriqueño and the University of Puerto Rico have promoted the study, appreciation, and dissemination of the Island's rich and diverse cultural traditions, including the Taíno background. Cultural (and especially linguistic) nationalism has created a strong ideological front against colonialism, even though it has not undermined the political and economic bases of the colonial discourse. The search for indigenous "roots" has added historical and geographic depth to national culture, apart from Spanish and U.S. influences. In the diaspora, Taíno symbolism has served to reassert Puerto Rican identity in a hostile environment. Today, most Puerto Ricans identify strongly, if somewhat superficially, with the Island's original inhabitants. Many feel a deep continuity between the past, present, and future of their collective selves, as suggested by the highly emotional use of the native terms Borinquen, *borinqueño, borincano,* and *boricua.*

On the negative side, the dominant image of the Puerto Rican nation as a harmonious integration of three cultures and races is problematic on both theoretical and political grounds. As Dávila (1997) and others have argued, the official view of national culture on the Island glosses over inner conflicts and bolsters the myth of a "racial democracy" based on *mestizaje.* According to this view, the Taínos and Africans fused imperceptibly with the Spanish to form a new cultural amalgam that overcame racial and ethnic fissures. And yet, a close analysis of both the hegemonic discourse and institutional practices on Puerto Rican identity reveals the systematic overvaluation of the Hispanic element, the romanticization of Taíno Indians, and the underestimation of African-derived ingredients. In the process of constructing their image of Puerto Ricanness, cultural nationalists have symbolically made Indians out of blacks. That is, they have often exaggerated the indigenous roots while neglecting the African contribution to the Island's largely mulatto population and hybrid culture.

Let us hope that future versions of the nationalist discourse develop broader and more inclusive ways of narrating the Puerto Rican nation.

References

Aguiló Ramos, Silvia
> (1987) *Idea y concepto de la cultura puertorriqueña durante la década del '50.* Ph.D. dissertation, Centro de Estudios Avanzados de Puerto Rico y el Caribe.

Alegría, Ricardo E.
> (n.d.) *The Museum of the Puerto Rican Indian.* San Juan: Institute of Puerto Rican Culture.
> (1950) *Historia de nuestros indios (versión elemental).* San Juan: Departamento de Instrucción.
> (1957) *La fiesta de Santiago Apóstol en Loíza Aldea.* San Juan: Colección de Estudios Puertorriqueños.
> (1971) *Los museos del Instituto de Cultura Puertorriqueña.* San Juan: Instituto de Cultura Puertorriqueña.
> (1978) Introducción: los estudios arqueológicos en Puerto Rico. *Revista/ Review Interamericana,* 8 (3): 380–385.
> (1996) *El Instituto de Cultura Puertorriqueña 1955–1973: 18 años contribuyendo a fortalecer nuestra conciencia nacional.* Second edition. San Juan: Instituto de Cultura Puertorriqueña.

Alvarez-Curbelo, Silvia, and María Elena Rodríguez Castro, eds.
> (1993) *Del nacionalismo al populismo: cultura y política en Puerto Rico.* Río Piedras, Puerto Rico: Ediciones Huracán.

Alvarez Nazario, Manuel
> (1974) *El elemento afronegroide en el español de Puerto Rico.* San Juan: Instituto de Cultura Puertorriqueña.
> (1992) *Historia de la lengua española en Puerto Rico.* San Juan: Academia Puertorriqueña de la Lengua Española.

Anderson, Benedict
> (1991) *Imagined Communities: Reflections on the Origins and Spread of Nationalism.* Second edition. London: Verso.

Asociación Puertorriqueña de Antropólogos y Arqueólogos
> (1990) *Arqueología de rescate: cinco ponencias.* San Juan: Asociación Puertorriqueña de Antropólogos y Arqueólogos.

Ayala-Richards, Haydée
> (1995) *La presencia de los taínos en la literatura puertorriqueña.* Ph.D. dissertation, University of Nebraska.

Babín, María Teresa

(1986) *La cultura de Puerto Rico.* Second edition. San Juan: Instituto de Cultura Puertorriqueña.

Bhabha, Homi K.

(1994) *The Location of Culture.* London: Routledge.

Bhabha, Homi K., ed.

(1990) *Nation and Narration.* London: Routledge.

Brau, Salvador

(1972) [1894] *Puerto Rico y su historia.* Second edition. San Juan: Editorial IV Centenario.

Buitrago Ortiz, Carlos

(1982) "Anthropology in the Puerto Rican Colonial Context: Analysis and Projections," in *Indigenous Anthropology in Non-Western Countries,* Hussein Fahim, ed, pp. 97–111. Durham, N.C.: Carolina Academic Press.

Chambers, Ian, and Linda Curti, eds.

(1996) *The Post-Colonial Question: Common Skies, Divided Horizons.* London: Routledge.

Chanlatte Baik, Luis A.

(1976) *Cultura igneri: investigaciones arqueológicas en Guayanilla, Puerto Rico.* Santo Domingo: Museo del Hombre Dominicano y Fundación García Arévalo.

(1986) *Cultura ostionoide: un desarrollo agroalfarero antillano.* San Juan: n.p.

(1990) *Nueva arqueología de Puerto Rico: su proyección en las Antillas.* Santo Domingo: Taller.

Chatterjee, Partha

(1993) *The Nation and its Fragments: Colonial and Postcolonial Histories.* Princeton: Princeton University Press.

(1995) *Nationalist Thought and the Colonial World: A Derivative Discourse?* Second edition. Minneapolis: University of Minnesota Press.

Coll y Toste, Cayetano

(1979) [1897] *Prehistoria de Puerto Rico.* Second edition. Cataño, Puerto Rico: Litografía Metropolitana.

Corchado Juarbe, Carmen

(1993) *El indio en la poesía puertorriqueña: desde 1847 hasta la generación del sesenta. Antología.* Second edition. Río Piedras, Puerto Rico: ESMACO.

Dávila, Arlene

(1994) "The Historical Development of the Taíno Indians as a Symbol of National Identity in Puerto Rico." Lecture in a course on Puerto Rican Culture, University of the Sacred Heart, Santurce, Puerto Rico.

(1997) *Sponsored Identities: Cultural Politics in Puerto Rico.* Philadelphia: Temple University Press.

Departamento de Educación (Puerto Rico) 1992 *Puerto Rico: museos, monumen-*

tos y lugares históricos. San Juan: Departamento de Educación.

Duany, Jorge

(1987) "Imperialistas reacios: los antropólogos norteamericanos en Puerto Rico, 1898–1950," *Revista del Instituto de Cultura Puertorriqueña*, 26 (97): 3–11.

Duncan, Ronald J.

(1978) "The Taínos as a Symbol of Cultural Identity," *Revista/Review* Interamericana, 8 (3): 500–510.

Fernández Méndez, Eugenio

(1972) *Art and Mythology of the Taíno Indians of the Greater West Indies.* San Juan: El Cemí.

(1980) *Puerto Rico: filiación y sentido de una isla.* San Juan: Ariel.

Flores Collazo, Margarita

(1998) "La lucha por definir la nación: el debate en torno a la creación del Instituto de Cultura Puertorriqueña, 1955," *Op.Cit.: Revista del Centro de Investigaciones Históricas*, 10: 175–200.

González, Lydia Milagros, ed.

(1993) *La tercera raíz: presencia africana en Puerto Rico.* San Juan: Centro de Estudios de la Realidad Puertorriqueña.

Harassym, Sarah, ed.

(1990) *The Post-Colonial Critic: Interviews, Strategies, Dialogues. Gayatri Chakravorty Spivak.* London: Routledge.

Hobsbawm, Eric J.

(1983) "Introduction: Inventing Traditions," in *The Invention of Tradition,* Eric J. Hobsbawm and Terence Ranger, eds, pp. 1–14. Cambridge, U.K.: Cambridge University Press.

Hostos, Adolfo de

(1941) *Anthropological Papers.* San Juan: Office of the Historian, Government of Puerto Rico.

Instituto de Cultura Puertorriqueña

(1997) *Ocho trabajos de investigación arqueológica en Puerto Rico.* San Juan: Instituto de Cultura Puertorriqueña.

Lloréns Torres, Luis

(1967) [1898] *América: estudios históricos y filosóficos sobre Puerto Rico.* Second edition. Hato Rey, Puerto Rico: Cordillera.

López-Baralt, Mercedes

(1985) *El mito taíno: Lévi-Strauss en las Antillas.* Second edition. Río Piedras, Puerto Rico: Ediciones Huracán.

López de Molina, Diana

(1980) "La arqueología como ciencia social," in *Crisis y crítica de las ciencias sociales en Puerto Rico,* Rafael R. Ramírez and Wenceslao Serra Deliz, eds, pp. 81–96. Río Piedras, Puerto Rico: Centro de Investigaciones Sociales,

Universidad de Puerto Rico.

López Sotomayor, Diana

(1975*) "Vieques: un momento de su historia."* M.A. thesis, Universidad Nacional Autónoma de México.

Marqués, René

(1977) *El puertorriqueño dócil y otros ensayos (1953–1971).* San Juan: Antillana.

Martínez-Echazábal, Lourdes

(1998) "Mestizaje and the Discourse of National/Cultural Identity in Latin America," *Latin American Perspectives*, 25 (3): 21–42.

Mason, Otis T.

(1877) *The Latimer Collection of Antiquities from Porto Rico in the National Museum at Washington, D.C.* Washington, D.C.: Government Printing Office.

Morales Cabrera, Pablo

(1932) *Puerto Rico indígena: prehistoria y protohistoria de Puerto Rico.* San Juan: Imprenta Venezuela.

Morris, Nancy

(1995) *Puerto Rico: Culture, Politics, and Identity.* New York: Praeger.

Moscoso, Francisco

(1986) *Tribus y clases en el Caribe antiguo.* San Pedro de Macorís, Dominican Republic: Universidad Central del Este.

Muñoz Marín, Luis

(1985) [1953] "La personalidad puertorriqueña en el Estado Libre Asociado," in *Del cañaveral a la fábrica: cambio social en Puerto Rico,* Eduardo Rivera Medina and Rafael L. Ramírez, eds, pp. 99–108. Río Piedras, Puerto Rico: Ediciones Huracán.

Radcliffe, Sarah, and Sallie Westwood

(1996) *Remaking the Nation: Place, Identity and Politics in Latin America.* London: Routledge.

Ramírez, Rafael L.

(1985) "El cambio, la modernización y la cuestión cultural," in *Del cañaveral a la caña: cambio social en Puerto Rico,* Eduardo Rivera Medina and Rafael L. Ramírez, eds, pp. 9–64. Río Piedras, Puerto Rico: Ediciones Huracán.

Rivera, Angel Israel

(1996) *Puerto Rico: ficción y mitología en sus alternativas de status.* San Juan: Nueva Aurora.

Roberts, Peter

(1997) "The (Re)Construction of the Concept of 'Indio' in the National Identities of Cuba, the Dominican Republic, and Puerto Rico," in *Caribe 2000: definiciones, identidades y culturas regionales y/o nacionales,* Lowell Fiet and Janette Becerra, eds, pp. 99–120. Río Piedras, Puerto Rico: Facultad de Humanidades, Universidad de Puerto Rico.

Rodríguez, Luisantonio
(1998) "Tibes: lugar enigmatico," *Notisur* (Ponce, Puerto Rico), January 17: 15–21.
Rodríguez, Miguel
(1984) *Estudio arqueológico del Valle del Río Cagüitas, Caguas, Puerto Rico.* Caguas: Museo de la Universidad del Turabo.
Rodríguez Olleros, Angel
(1974) *Canto a la raza: composición sanguínea de estudiantes de la Universidad de Puerto Rico.* Río Piedras, Puerto Rico: Colegio de Farmacia, Universidad de Puerto Rico.
Rouse, Irving B.
(1992) *The Taínos: The Rise and Decline of the People who Greeted Columbus.* New Haven: Yale University Press.
Routté-Gómez, Eneid
(1995) "A Conspiracy of Silence: Racism in Puerto Rico." *San Juan City Magazine,* 4 (8): 54–58.
Stahl, Agustín
(1889) *Los indios borinqueños: estudios etnográficos.* San Juan: Imprenta Librería de Acosta.
Sued Badillo, Jalil
(1978) *Los caribes: ¿realidad o fábula?* Río Piedras, Puerto Rico: Antillana.
(1995a) "The Island Caribs: New Approaches to the Question of Ethnicity in the Early Colonial Caribbean," in *Wolves from the Sea: Readings in the Anthropology of the Native Caribbean,* Neil L. Whitehead, ed, pp. 61–89. Leiden: KITLV Press.
(1995b) "The Theme of the Indigenous in the National Projects of the Hispanic Caribbean," in *Making Alternative Histories: The Practice of Archaeology and History in Non-Western Settings,* Peter R. Schmidt and Thomas C. Patterson, eds, pp. 25–46. Santa Fe, New Mexico: School of American Research Press.
Thomas, Nicholas
(1994) *Colonialism's Culture: Anthropology, Travel, and Government.* Princeton: Princeton University Press.
Vizcarrondo, Alicia
(1994) *Puerto Rico, mi gran comunidad.* Río Piedras, Puerto Rico: Cultural Panamericana.
Wade, Peter
(1997) *Race and Ethnicity in Latin America.* London: Pluto.
Williams, Patrick, and Laura Chrisman, eds.
(1994) *Colonial Discourse and Post-Colonial Theory: A Reader.* New York: Columbia University Press.

The mural *Mi cultura* with Taíno motifs.
(photo by Arlene Dávila)

PELÍCULA HECHA EN PUERTO RICO
por la División de Educación de la Comunidad
Departamento de Instrucción Pública

Idealized Taínos in the poster *La buena herencia*.
(photo by Arlene Dávila)

Woman in indigenous costume with peacock feather and *guiro*
at the Taíno festival in Jayuya, Puerto Rico.
(photo by Arlene Dávila)

Children dressed as Taínos: some wearing wigs.
(photo by Arlene Dávila)

Taíno Queen at the 1995 National Indigenous Festival: Jayuya, Puerto Rico.
(photo by Holger Thoss)

Taíno dance at the 1995 Festival: Jayuya, Puerto Rico.
(photo by Holger Thoss)

Procession of participants in Taíno festival: Maricao, Puerto Rico.
(photo by Holger Thoss)

Taíno cleansing ceremony: Utuado, Puerto Rico.
(photo by Holger Thoss)

4.

PETER ROBERTS

What's in a Name, an Indian Name?

When William Shakespeare had Juliet ask the question "What's in a name?" and then replied in anguish, saying "That which we call a rose by any other name would smell as sweet," he was really highlighting the fact that names do matter. The tragedy of *Romeo and Juliet* is precisely the matter of names and the fact that Juliet is a Capulet and Romeo is a Montague. In order to overcome the circumstances of their birth and avert the problems that they were facing, Juliet says: "I'll no longer be a Capulet" and Romeo in like manner responds: "Henceforth, I never will be Romeo." Presumably, after relinquishing their own names, they would have been compelled to choose other names. This method of trying to overcome the circumstances of one's birth is very human, but the solving of problems is not always the basis for relinquishing a name or adopting the name of another.

The tradition of choosing a different identity or adopting another name seems to be evident across all human societies. It is evident both in everyday life and also in more temporary and dramatic ways. For example, at certain festivals, people don masks, give themselves other names, and temporarily parade their different identities in public. In the Caribbean islands in the context of colonialism, choosing to be another or adopting the name of another has had a stronger impetus than in many other areas of the world. The major practice or manifestation of this tradition in the Caribbean has been to choose to be racially white and to adopt white names. The literature on the Caribbean is full of this. Outside the Spanish-American world, the tradition of choosing to be an Indian or accepting an Indian name may not be as well known. Generally, except at festivals such as carnival, and in most cases outside the Spanish-speaking Caribbean, playing the part of an Indian at a party, a game, or some other social event means that the person is acting out and perpetuating the society's negative values and beliefs about Indians. By contrast, adopting an Indian name in the Spanish-speaking Caribbean has a long history and the reasons for it vary in relation to the perceived image of the Indian. By examining the terms used and their application, one can see how the practice of adopting the name of another became a tradition in the Spanish-speaking Caribbean.

First of all, the very word "Indian," as applied to the people of the New World by the Europeans of the 16th century, was the earliest case of name transference from one people or race to that of another. It was the result of a reasonable conclusion at the time that it was done, for as Sued Badillo says:

> Columbus found innumerable clues to suggest that the Caribbean was the Indian Ocean and its islands those described by Marco Polo or attributed to him. (Sued Badillo 1995: 75)

Besides the fact that conclusions were based on limited geographical knowledge, the transfer of the term "Indian" to the Americas was also based on the belief that there were cannibals in the Indies: a belief that was confirmed at the time by reports about the Caribs. Another reason had to do with the skin color of people. This is stated by Peter Martyr, who, in an account translated by Richard Eden in 1555, said:

> Some think that the people of the New World were called Indians because they are of the color of the East Indians. (Martyr 1555: 311)

Thus, because the Caribs were identified as cannibals and because they were described as olive-skinned, they became Indians for the Europeans.

Even after it became clear that the New World was not India, and in spite of the fact that no genetic link was ever established between the Indians of the Old World and the Indians of the New World, both continued to be called Indians and writers continued to mention the similarity in skin color and color and texture of hair, even up to the 20th century, thereby continuing to suggest some validation of the name "Indian" for both.

Within the New World, but much later, the name "Indian" was applied to yet another racial group. In the Dominican Republic, the term *indio* was officially adopted to describe the black or mixed population of that country. This was really the result of a development that started even before the revolution in neighboring Haiti or St. Domingue. For example, in 1767, Louis XV issued a decree aimed at controlling the *gens de couleur* in St. Domingue and denying them the privileges of whites. In this policy decision, Louis XV made a blanket statement excluding all blacks and their descendants from parity with whites, but he also said:

> *ceux qui proviennent d'une race indienne doivent être assimilés aux sujets du Roi.*

As a result of this decree, and others issued by the Spanish crown, many people subsequently chose to become the descendants of Indians on the island of Hispaniola, especially on the eastern or Dominican side of the island. The purpose of becoming an Indian in the Dominican case was two-fold; to avoid exclusion from the white world and to avoid being associated with the black world of Haiti. In the Dominican Republic, at the intellectual and political level, the Indian was systematically imposed on the people as a racial category, and *indio* became a general racial type replacing the black category and all its derivatives. In this context, *indio* became a euphemism for non-white Dominicans, who were thus disconnected from the Haitians and the legacy of slavery and sugar production in that society. In summary, the term "Indian" could be used in the Dominican Republic to refer to three racial types—Native Americans, Indians from India, and Blacks and mulattos in Dominican society.

Another instance of the use of one term for different races, in this case within the context of the New World, was the word "Carib." The word

85

"Caraiba," in the early years, was used as a name for both the native inhabitants of the Eastern Caribbean and the Europeans who settled there, because it was a common noun. More than a hundred years after the colonization process began, Joannes De Laet (1640 [1633]), though accepting *Caribe* as a common name for the indigenous inhabitants of the small Caribbean islands, continued to support a point that was originally made by Americo Vespucci, who said:

> ...*Caraiba (que quelques-uns on pris pour un Enchanteur)*
> *signifie la puissance par laquelle se font les miracles, voila*
> *purquoi ils ont nommé les Portugais, & les nomment encore*
> *aujourd'hui Caraiba, pource qu'ils faisoyent beaucoup de*
> *choses qui surpassoyent leur entendement.*

De Laet, at that point, was talking about an ethnic group in Brazil. The *quelques-uns* whom he was referring to (in the quotation above) was specifically Andre Thevet, who by explanation and elaboration (1575: 913) compared *Caribe* to *prophetes*. It is not clear from this and the preceding works, whether both words (*Caraibes* and *Caribes/Canibales*) were thought to be variants of the same original word. In any case, this use of the word *caraiba/caribe* to refer to both the Europeans and the Indians was a matter of ignorance on the part of Europeans writers—more so than conscious choice or adoption.

Another outstanding early case of the transfer of a term of identification from one race or ethnic group to another involved the word *guatiao*. In the early colonies, in contrast to the native inhabitants who conjured up the vision of wild people who ate humans (i.e. the Caribs), there were those who had come to be identified as guatiaos or docile peaceful natives. Citing evidence from the *Nueva Biblioteca de Autores*, Pedro Henriquez Ureña (1938: 96, note 1), says that from early in the century, the term *guatiao* had come into common usage.

> *En 1516 ya usan la palabra guatiao come genérica los*
> *padres Jerónimos que gobernaban las Indias desde Santo*
> *Domingo.*

Henriquez Ureña (1938: 96, note 1) also points to evidence in the *Coleción de documentos...de Indias* that a difference had developed between those native inhabitants called *caribes* and those called *guatiaos*.

In Martyr's division of the natives in the islands, those who welcomed the Europeans were called, not *guatiaos*, but *Taíni*. In the *First Decade*, Martyr actually used the term "Taíno" and gives as its meaning (Martyr 1555: 4) "a good man" and (Martyr 1555: 9) "noble men." In the latter case he makes a contrast between the *Taíni* on the one hand and the *Canibales* on the other. So, *Taíni* and *guatiaos* essentially referred to the same people.

Las Casas, in his account of the early encounters between Indians and the Spanish, said:

> *A éste, como al señor principal y señalado, el capitán general dio su nombre, trocándolo por el suyo, diciendo que se llamase adelante Juan de Esquivel, y que él se llamaría Cotubano, como él. Este trueque de nombres en la lengua común desta isla se llamaba ser yo y fulano, que trocamos los nombres, guatiaos, y así se llamaba el uno al otro guatiao. Teníase por gran parentesco y como liga de perpetua amistad y confederación. Y así el capitán general y aquel señor quedaron guatiaos, como perpetuos amigos y hermanos en armas. Y así los indios llamaban Cotubano al capitán, y al señor, Juan de Esquivel.* (Las Casas 1986 [1542]: 2, 37)

So, by this exchange of names, noted by Las Casas, and by the use of the word *guatiao*, the Indians conferred native status (citizenship) on the Spaniards. The stated object of the exchange of names between the *guatiaos* and the Spaniards was to establish a bond of friendship.

Another case of name transfer was the use of the words *guajiro* and *jibaro* in Cuba and Puerto Rico respectively. In Cuba, the term *guajiro* emerged as a euphemism for peasant or farmer. The *guajiro* were essentially rural and tied to the land, as Pichardo y Tapia (1976 [1875]: 296) explained:

87

...en la Isla de Cuba, principalmente en la parte occidental es mui comun y distinta su significacion. Aquí Guajiro es sinónimo de Campesino, esto es, la persona dedicada al campo con absoluta residencía en él...

The name *guajiro* was recognized as a word that originated with the indigenous inhabitants of the region, but the geographical origin of the *guajiros* was a source of controversy among 19th-century academics in Cuba. One of these academics, Antonio Bachiller y Morales, thought that he had the answer. Using the work of the Italian Codazzi on Venezuela as one of his sources, he argued (1883: 109):

Encontramos en el continente un tribu numerosa de indios llamados guagiros, existe una peninsula que lleva el nombre de la Goayira. Es, pues, evidente, que de ese punto hubimos el nombre.

He was talking about the "Guahiros" of Venezuela, who were at the time well known for their business skills as well as their opposition to the Spaniards. Bachiller y Morales (1883: 109–110) then proceeded to account for the application of the name to Cubans who were descendants of Europeans:

¿pero qué tienen de comun con los indios de continente, hombres descendientes de Europa? ¿se llamaron así los cubanos alguna vez?—Creemos que si supiésemos el signifi-cado de la palabra, fácilmente resolveríamos la cuestion. Peor si acudimos á anologías, desde luego podemos decir que los indios llamaron guagiros á nuestros campesinos, por reconocer que eran semejantes á estos seres que sostenian un activo comercio con todas las islas, y que aún en la actu-alidad se les reputa por uno de los más inteligentes é indus-triosos naturales. ...y los aborígenes que vieron una raza de más poder moral é inteligencia, no pudieron dejar de hacer comparaciones con objetos que les eran conocidos.

Bachiller y Morales clearly regarded this as a case of the native inhabitants giving a name to the descendants of Europeans (*hombres descendientes de Europa*) in Cuba. The purpose of the naming here was therefore the same as in the case of *Caraiba*, the application of a known name to another group in order to highlight similarities.

However, contrary to what most of the literature suggested, Bachiller y Morales argued that the Cuban *campesino* was insulted by being called by an Indian name:

> *Los habitantes del campo aún se molestan en el dia de que se les llame guagiros... De esto mismo puede creerse que nace la odiosidad con que nuestros campesinos repugnan el nombre. Nuestros padres no querian verse comparar con los indios bravos."* (1883: 109–110).

This, no doubt, was an end of the century interpretation of a development that had taken place at a much earlier time in Cuban history, for there is no indication of this attitude in the definition of *guajiro* in Esteban Pichardo's dictionary, the earliest version of which appeared in the first half of the 19th century. Apparently, feelings of racial superiority had become so deeply entrenched in Cuba among whites in the last half of the century that no white could be admitted to have willingly adopted an Indian name. Yet, at the same time, Indians were believed to be a part of the genetic make-up of the Cuban population. Bachiller y Morales (1883: 108) did not even question the idea of Indian genetic survival in contemporary Cubans when he said:

> *Parece que estábamos condenados á no llegar al conocimiento de estas cosas por la confusion de las dos razas española é indiana que hoy forman una sola...*

The term *guajiro* may originally have been a very positive one for the rural population, but for some intellectuals and the sophisticates it was clearly not.

Another case of name adoption is the use of *siboney* to identify Cubans in the 19th century. The *Siboney* were recreated from history as brave and noble warriors. However, some people actually believed that they could still find people of Indian ancestry in those parts of Cuba (Guanabacoa, Caney, and Jiguani), where the indigenous inhabitants had survived the longest (Turnbull 1969 [1840]: 233). Interestingly enough, in view of the fact that the *guajiro* (an originally foreign Indian name) had become a stereotype in contemporary Cuba, there was a certain precision and accuracy in the identification of the Cuban Indian as *siboney* in the poetry of the early and mid-19th century. Max Henríquez Ureña (1963: 1, 174) regards *ciboneyismo* as the bringing together of two traditions—la tendencia indianista and la tendencia criollista:

> El ciboneyismo no era más que una manifestación de la ten-
> dencia indianista, que ya para entonces estaba difundida en
> la América española como una rama del americanismo lit-
> erario, y a ella habían respondido en Cuba: José María
> Heredia, con su poema. Las sombras…; y Plácido con los
> romances Cora y Jicotencal. Lo que hizo Fornaris, al cir-
> cunscribir esa tendencia dentro del ámbito de Cuba, fue
> darle un nombre local y exclusivo.
>
> Dentro de sus composiciones combinó Fornaris, no
> siempre con fortuna, palabras y nombres indígenas, como si
> de ese modo pudiera dar carta de naturaleza ciboney a sus
> versos, pero las escenas y costumbres que aspira a pintar no
> se diferencian más que en el vocabulario de las que la ten-
> dencia simplemente criollista señala en el guajiro, que nada
> tiene de indígena.

Athough Henríquez Ureña identified the contradiction between what was Cuban in name, what was Spanish American in reality, and what was Indian in name, but non-indigenous in substance, he did not highlight the contradiction between the name *siboney,* which was truly Cuban historical-ly but as a recreation seemed false, and the name *guajiro,* which was not the name of Cuban Indians, but which had become a symbol for Cuban national identity.

Ciboneyismo is also analyzed as a method of circumventing the harsh censorship in Cuba in the 19th century. As such, it was not a romanticization of the past but a way of criticizing the contemporary political situation by making it seem as if one was referring to the historical conflict between the Spaniards and the native inhabitants. This was done especially by those who did not have the safety and freedom of being in another country and having their work published outside of Cuba. This point is made by Remos y Rubio (1958: 119):

> *Era una forma indirecta de expresar las angustias de la patria, recordando las angustias y persecuciones de los indios; los autores vivían en Cuba, y no tenían la facilidad y despreocupación que podían gozar los desterrados.*

Ciboneyismo was not considered to be good literature, but it was very popular in Cuba in the middle of the 19th century. Its success is explained as the result of a combination of factors, but especially as a result of the political reality:

> *La ingenuidad de su alegorismo, el amor por la naturaleza cubana y sobre todo las evidentes connotaciones políticos de aquellos poemas en aquellos momentos de férrea censura, explican su éxito."* (ILLACC 1983: 256).

The words of the poem *La Bayamesa* by Pedro Figueredo, ostensibly exhorting the Indian *bayameses* to throw off the Spanish yoke and to free Cuba, were turned into lyrics and became the most famous song of the revolutionary period in the 19th century (1868–1898). The first two stanzas of the same poem are now the national anthem of Cuba. *Ciboneyismo* therefore provided a strong image that linked the 16th century *siboney* to the 19th-century Cuban in their fight against the Spanish oppressor and has survived into the 20th century.

While for intellectuals (i.e., as a result of research), the Indian had been re-created with "accurate" names (e.g., *siboney*), at the popular level, the Indian names which had become common (*guajiro, jíbaro*) were difficult to expain and justify as native to Cuba and Puerto Rico, so much so that there were attempts to give them a European origin. Paradoxically then, the *criollo* in Cuba and Puerto Rico took on a contradictory ethnic aspect through both intellectual and popular adoption and the use of specific Indian names. The *criollo*, as if by absorbing the characteristics of the Indian, had changed ethnically without becoming Indian.

It was not only names applied to one race that were adopted by other races or transferred from one to another, but also names that had developed to identify the mixture of races. It is the Spanish who were credited with having developed a gradient system from the racial mixtures of people in the New World, and it was in relationship to European-Indian mixtures that it was initiated. Early evidence of what was to develop into an elaborate system can be found in the *Comentarios Reales* of the Peruvian, Garcilaso de la Vega. In the chapter *Nombres nuevos para nombrar diversas generaciones*, Garcilaso said:

> *A los hijos de español y de mestiza, o de mestizo y española, llaman cuatralvos, por decir que tienen cuarta parte de indio y tres de español. A los hijos de mestizo y de india, o de indio y de mestizo, llaman tresalvos, por decir que tienen tres partes de indio y una de español. Todos estos nombres y otros, que por excusar hastío dejamos de decir, se han inventado en mi tierra para nombrr las generaciones que ha habido despues que los españoles fueron a ella...."* (BAE 1963: 133, 373–374)

The words *cuatralvos* and *tresalvos* have the ending—*alvo* which presumably is the same as *-avo* at the end of the word *octavo*, identifying a fraction or "part." Contrary to what Garcilaso's explanation suggests, the terms *cuatralvos* and *tresalvos* gave only the percentage of Indian blood that the individual had. So, it was not simply that the Spanish intended to give a mathematical precision to the racial composition of individuals, it was that they wanted to highlight the amount of non-white blood the individual was supposed to have in an ordinal or hierarchical fashion.

A later and more developed gradient system was explained in the context of Jamaica by the Englishman, Edward Long (1970 [1774]: 2, 260–261) in the following way:

The intermixture of Whites, Blacks, and Indians, has generated several different casts, which have all their proper denominations, invented by the Spaniards, who make this a kind of science among them. Perhaps they will be better understood by the following table.

DIRECT lineal Ascent from the Negroe Venter

White Man, = Negroe Woman.
|
White Man, = *Mulatta.*
|
White Man, = *Terceron.*
|
White Man, = *Quateron.*
|
White Man, = *Quinteron.*
|
White

Mediate or Stationary, neither advancing nor receding

Quateron, = Terceron
|
Tente en el ayre.

Retrograde

Mulatto,= Terceron.	Negroe,= *Mulatta.*	Indian,= *Mulatta.*	Negroe,= Indian.
|	|	|	|
Saltatras.	*Sambo de* = Negroe. Mulatta,	*Mestize.*	*Sambo de = Sambo de* Indian, *Mulatta.*
	|		|
	Negroe.		*Givero.**

*(Perhaps from *gifero*, a butcher)

93

The basic (top part of the) gradient system identified the percentage of black/African background that characterized individuals of black/white mixture. This was seen to be necessary in the gradient system, for becoming white, that is, getting rid of non-white blood, was seen as the purpose of "lineal ascent," as Long (1970 [1774]: 2, 261) explained:

> In the Spanish colonies, it is accounted most creditable to
> mend the breed by ascending or growing whiter....

In contrast to the "direct lineal ascent" or growing "whiter," there were the "mediate" or "stationary" types, "neither advancing nor receding" and others still that were "retrograde," meaning that the offspring were headed towards blackness. The terminology used to identify the "mediate" and "retrograde" types was not of the mathematical type but of common words with extended meanings. The system as a whole therefore combined precise and imprecise terms along a continuum and, in the words of Long, was a "kind of science" among the Spaniards.

The French and the English adopted the gradient system of color and race, together with most of the actual terms, from the Spanish and so the gradient system and the values attached to it became pervasive throughout all of the European colonies. In the system given by Long, persons who had less than one fifth of black blood were considered white in the Spanish colonies. Long claimed, however, that in Jamaica the English system was not as exclusive as the Spanish system, allowing anyone who was "above three degrees removed in lineal descent from the Negro ancestor" to count as white. The Dutch, however, were different, according to Long; they were the most extreme/exclusive of all the colonial nations in the matter of lineal ascent or the attainment of whiteness:

> The Dutch, I am informed, transcend the Spaniards very
> far in their refinement of these complexions. They add
> drops of pure water to a single drop of dusky liquor, until
> it becomes tolerably pellucid. But this needs the apposi-
> tion of such multitude of drops, that, to apply the experi-
> ment by analogy to the human race, twenty or thirty gen-
> erations, perhaps, would hardly be sufficient to discharge
> the stain. (Long 1774: 2, 261).

Long failed to discuss the actual details of the Dutch system of classification, but it was probably little different from the French colonial system given by Moreau de Saint Méry, which did not allow for the recovery
of whiteness through "lineal ascent:" a fact that was reinforced by Louis
XV's decision of 1767. Therefore, though white was not a practical, achiev-
able classification in the French and Dutch colonies, it was in the Spanish,
and concerted attempts were made at the personal and the national levels
to achieve it.

No doubt it was practically impossible to keep separate the great number of racially mixed types that came into being, but the fact that the gradient or hierarchical classification was mentioned in most descriptions
attests to its abiding importance in the identification of people for practical social purposes. The sliding scale of privileges, which was the essential
reason for the hierarchical classification, was topped by whiteness, which
carried the greatest privileges. This is evident in the following subjective,
nationalistic remark by Long, who was trying to show that the English
were less exclusive than the other European nations:

> These distinctions, however, do not prevail in Jamaica; for
> here the Terceron is confounded with the Quateron; and
> the laws permit all, that are above three degrees removed
> in lineal descent from the Negro ancestor, to vote at elec-
> tions and enjoy all the privileges and immunities of his
> majesty's white subjects of the island. (Long 1970 [1774]:
> 2, 261)

As this remark makes clear, the gradient hierarchy was not just a system of social value: it was also part of the legal system. Racial distinctions
and terminology became so entrenched in the minds and actions of people
in the colonies that they were almost immutable and became bulwarks
against social mobility and supports which retained privilege.

In the Spanish colonies, as well as in the others, since entitlements of
succession and privileges of association were accorded legally and officially according to the percentage of blood that an individual had, it was the
pseudo-mathematical terms (e.g., *tresalvo, cuatralvo*; *quateron, quinteron*)
which were used to facilitate this. In St. Domingue, where the *gens de*

95

couleur increasingly resented the attempts of whites to restrict their privileges, the legislation of the 18th century (e.g., Louis XVI's 1767 decree) in large measure led to the Haitian Revolution of 1791. Yet, in everyday social interaction between people, the pseudo-mathematical terms were not the more common of the two types—it was the more subjective terms which were more common. It was these non-white terms, which facilitated confusion, extension, and transfer.

Among the subjective terms were the Indian names, which, because of the ambivalent values accorded to the Indian, as well as the historical use of Indian terms by other racial groups, were transferred across racial types, thereby acquiring double and extended values. The following are some of the actual Indian terms or terms applied to Indians or Indian mixtures that ʷʳe given by Long, Moreau de Saint-Méry, and others, as well as their extensions in meaning:

Mestizo = Spanish + Indian (Garcilaso de la Vega 1963 [1609])
  Mestize = Indian + *mulatta* (Long 1970 [1774])
  Moustiches = *Nègre* + *Indienne* (Fermin 1769)
  Métis = *Blanc* + *Quarteron* (1/8 negro blood)
  Mustee = White + Quadroon

Mameluco = Indian + White
  Mamelouque = *Blanc* + *métive* (1/16 negro blood)

Caboclo = White + Indian
  caboclo = mulatto with kinky hair (Brazil)
  candomblé caboclo = African & Indian *candomblé* (Brazil)
  cabougles = *Negre* + *Mulatresse* (3/4 negro blood)
    (Fermin 1769)

Marabá (Brazil). *Pessoa mestiça de índio e branco*
  marabou = *Mulatre* + *Griffonne/Sacatra;*
  marabou = *Negre* + *Quarteronne*

Cafuso = Negro + Indian

Givero = *sambo de* Indian + *sambo de* mulatto (Long 1970 [1774])
   xíbaro = *cafufuso* + *negro*
   [*grifo* = *hijo de indio y loba*
   griffe = *negre* + *mulatresse; negre* + *marabou*
   grifo – *Dicese de los cabellos crespos o enmarañados.*
      En Mexico y Puerto Rico, pelo pasudo, el ensortijado de los
      negros. En Cuba, persona de color.
   grinfo – Negro in Brazil
   grifonne – in the French colonies
   Garifuna "Black Carib" in St. Vincent]

Etymological Sources

mestizo/mestize/moustiche/métis/mustee<mixtus (Latin)
caboclo/cabougle<caboco, caboculo, caboclo (Brazilian Tupi)
marabou<marbá (Brazilian Indian)
mameluco/mamelouque<mamaruca (Brazilian Tupi and also of
   Egyptian Arabic origin)
cafuso
givero/xíbaro (South American Indian)
[*grifo/grinfo/griffe/grifonne*<Greek *griphos* (*"encorvado, retorcido;"*
   "kinky hair")
   grinfa = *grenha, gaforina*
   grenha = entangled, long or matted hair; *Gaforina* = mop, shock
   (of hair)]

For reasons of politeness and euphemism as well as to access privileges, terms were extended beyond their presumed "accurate" reference. As a result, Indian terms of identity came to be used to refer to individuals who only looked like Indians. Color was the major feature of most of the terms as they became more stylized and especially when the terms were applied to areas where the population composition differed from that where the terms had their source. The White + Black mixtures were equated with the color of the White + Indian mixtures so that the color was kept more or less constant. For example, *mestizo* became the French term *moustiche*, which, especially in the context of French Louisiana, became the North American "mustee." In other words, *métis* (mustee), which was White + Indian was assessed to be the same color as White + *Quateron*.

The terms which identified Indian mixtures were Old World (e.g., *mestizo*< Latin *mixtus* "mixed") or Brazilian/South American Indian, non-specific, non-technical terms which obviously acquired specific references. The terms that came from South America most likely traveled with the sugar technology of the 17th century and with the slave trade from Brazil to the islands. So while the Spanish were identified as the ones who had developed the gradient system or classification, it is clear that some of the terms came from Brazil and that it was in the Portuguese, French, and Dutch settlements that words flourished in order to identify mixtures and colors of people.

All this transferring of Indian names to other racial/ethnic groups attests to the differing and sometimes ambivalent status that the Indian had in the European colonies of the New World. Generally, the Indian was subjected to degradation and abuse by the Europeans. However, in Europe from as early as the 16th century, the "noble savage" of the New World was put forward as a contrast to the decadent European. Las Casas argued, for example, that Indians were too fragile to do the arduous work required by the Spanish, while Louis XV accorded full status to the Indians and their descendants in the French colonies. Discussions of race generated by the colonization of the New World established a scale for humanity with the white European at the top and the black African at the bottom, with enlightenment at one end and darkness at the other. Consequently, European (white) and African (black) became polar extremes in the colonial structure in the Caribbean, which was characterized by sharp stratification at all levels in between. The Indian did not have a clear and uniform status in this scale. Therefore, Indian terms allowed for a variable and ambivalent status.

The survival instinct is said to be one of the strongest in humans and even more generally in animals. Nature is full of examples of adaptation to suit the environment, and it is Charles Darwin who is best known for expounding this theory. For example, the chameleon has become very well known for its adaptive characteristics. The chameleon changes the color of its skin both as a defense mechanism and as a mechanism to access privilege. Human beings cannot change the color of their skin (although many have tried) but they can change the clothes that cover their skin and they can change their names to suit the context. For instance, many Jews changed their names to avoid persecution and death and many Europeans (Italians, Poles, etc.) changed their names in the United States in order to avoid prejudice and discrimination. Human beings are known for constructing their own realities depending on time and context. This is especially so when they are uprooted from their traditional homes or are invaded by more powerful people. Therefore, in relation to the Caribbean, whether it was the Indians that the Europeans decimated, or the Europeans who were in unfamiliar lands, or the Africans who were uprooted from their homes—all of them had to construct or reconstruct an identity for themselves in the new environment. Name changing and adoption of names has been and continues to be a part of this. They had to do this both as a defense mechanism and as a way of accessing rights and privileges. It is no different for those who have migrated from the Caribbean to the great metropolises of North America and Europe in recent years.

References

Bachiller y Morales, Don Antonio
> (1883) *Cuba primitiva. Origen, lenguas, tradiciones e historia de los indios de las Antillas Mayores y Las Lucayas. 2da. edición.* Habana: Libreria de Miguel de Villa.

De Laet, Joannes
> (1640) [1633] *L'histoire du nouveau monde ou Description Des Indes Occidentales.* Leyde: Chez Bonaventure & Abraham Elseviers, Imprimeurs ordinaires de l'Universite.

Fermin, Phillippe
> (1769) *Description générale, historique, géographique et physique de la colonie de Surinam.* Amsterdam: E. van Harrevelt.

Garcilaso de la Vega, El Inca
> (1963) [1609] *Obras completas del Inca Garcilaso de la Vega II.* Biblioteca de Autores Españoles, vol. 133. Madrid: Ediciones Atlas, 1963.

Henríquez Ureña, Pedro
> (1938) *Para la historia de los indigenismos.* Buenos Aires: Universidad de Buenos Aires.

Henríquez Ureña, Max

(1963) *Panorama histórico de la literatura cubana*. 2 vols. New York: Las Americas Publishing Co.

ILLACC (Instituto de literatura y linguistica de la academia de ciencias de Cuba)

(1983) *Perfil histórico de las letras cubanas desde los orígenes hasta 1898.* Habana: Editorial Letras Cubanas.

Las Casas, Bartolomé

(1986) [1542] *Historia de las Indias*. 3 vols. Caracas: Biblioteca Ayacucho.

Long, Edward

(1970) [1774] *The History of Jamaica, or General Survey of the Ancient and Modern state of that island: with reflections on its Situations, Settlements, Inhabitants, Climate, Products, Commerce, Laws and Government.* London: Frank Cass.

Martyr, Peter

(1555) [1533] *The Decades of the newe worlde or west India.* Translated by Rycharde Eden. London: William Powell.

Moreau de Saint-Méry, M.L.E.

(1958) [1797] *Description topographieque, physique, civile, politique et historique de la Partie française de l'isle Saint-Domingue.* Paris: Société de l'histoire des colonies françaises.

Pichardo y Tapia, Esteban

(1976) [1875] *Diccionario provincial casi-razonado de vozes y frases cubanas.* Habana: Editorial de Ciencias Sociales.

Remos y Rubio, Juan Nepomuceno José.

(1958) *Proceso historico de las letras cubanas*. Madrid: Ediciones Guadarrama.

Sued Badillo, Jalil

(1995) "The Island Caribs: New approaches to the question of ethnicity in the early colonial Caribbean," in *Wolves from the Sea. Readings in the Anthropology of the Native Caribbean*, Neil N. Whitehead, ed. pp. 61–89. Leiden: KITLV Press.

Thevet, André

(1575) *La cosmographie universelle d'André Thevet, cosmographe du roi.* Paris: G. Chaudiere.

Turnbull, David

(1969) [1840] *Travels in the West. Cuba; with Notices of Porto Rico, and the Slave Trade.* New York: Negro Universities Press.

5.

MIRIAM JIMÉNEZ ROMÁN

The Indians are Coming!
The Indians are Coming!
The Taíno and Puerto Rican Identity*

> Who are my people? What tribe do I belong to? When I go to
> Puerto Rico, I am told that I am not Puerto Rican but
> American. In the States, I am not accepted among Spanish-
> speaking Latinos because of [my] inability to speak the lan-
> guage. Among African Americans I am not embraced as being
> among my own kind. And so I struggle, wanting to be part of
> my heritage, wanting to go "home," however I find myself alone,
> abandoned and hurting immensely.
>
> Little Lost Taíno[1]

Until very recently, Puerto Rico's Taínos were only spoken of in the
past tense, their present significance defined almost exclusively in symbolic
terms. Although there is a relatively extensive literature (most of it dating
from the mid-nineteeth century) and a continuing archeological and
ethnohistorical scholarly interest in the Taíno, all colonial and contemporary documentation attests to the virtual extinction of the Taínos

*This chapter is a revised version of a presentation offered on February 28, 1998, in the panel
"Rethinking Taíno: the Cultural Politics of the Use of their Legacy and Imagery," a public program
held in conjuction with the exhibition, Taíno, Pre-Columbian Art and Culture, at New York City's El
Museo del Barrio.

within fifty years of Spanish colonization of the island. Nevertheless, a revivalist movement, ostensibly inspired by the commemorative activities surrounding the quincentennial of the first voyage of Christopher Columbus to the "New World," suggests that the Taínos are not safely ensconced in historical oblivion. The Taíno has been resurrected and neither historical documentation nor simple logic can easily dismiss a movement that is gathering converts daily.

It is not mere happenstance that a Taíno resurgence comes precisely at a time when Puerto Ricans on both sides of the *charco* are seriously engaging the African foundations of island society and, more specifically, the role of race and racism in contemporary social relations. This newer Taíno movement can be viewed as both a variation on the same theme and as a backlash. On the one hand, the new Taínos are simply emphasizing one component of the official racial triad—that is, Puerto Ricans as a blend of Spanish, African and Taíno—and thus they appear as legitimate and relatively unthreatening to the status quo. While bearing little practical relevance to Puerto Rican daily life, the Taíno still serves the ideological function of qualifying the Spanish and African components of the racial triad, making Puerto Ricans, in a sense, "uniquely" Puerto Rican. At the same time, this privileging of the indigenous roots of Puerto Rican society is consistent with a long history of identification with Latin America, a Latin America where Indians are a tangible and recognized presence and Africans and their descendants have been effectively minimized or erased from the national picture.[2]

The tangible and recognized presence of Indians has, nevertheless, been traditionally conceived as a problem by most, if not all, Latin American nations. Explicitly through coercive and "persuasive" campaigns, and implicitly through marginalization of those who resist, the *indio* has been encouraged to assimilate culturally.[3] *Negros*, on the other hand, are presumed to already be culturally assimilated but still a problem that can only be rectified through biological "whitening."[4] While both racialized groups are discriminated against, it is the *indio* who is seen as truly representative of resistance to Western cultural dominance. Within the colonial/racial context of Puerto Rican society, the no longer tangible but nonetheless recognized Taíno becomes the symbol of uncorrupted integrity, the stalwart defender of the nation at its purest.

Beyond the symbolic aspect, however, for the new Taínos, as for those who emphasize the African component, the colonial relationship with the United States adds another vital dimension, one characterized by the more direct impact on Puerto Ricans—*aquí y allá*—of contemporary ideas, movements and legislation emanating from the metropole. Just as the *indio* construct of Latin America is selectively invoked, so too does the United States discourse receive a new twist in the colonial tangle. Rather than mirroring the metropole's perspective, the Puerto Rican engagement responds to its own dynamic, adapting elements which are congruent with the particular experiences and ideological exigencies of Puerto Rican communities within and beyond the national borders. Whether and how these trends are embraced or rejected is always influenced by the colonial relationship, so that environmentalism, sexuality, feminism, identity politics and "Latino-ness," anti-racism, and other post-Civil Rights movement developments take on a different cast, their meaning subject to the complexities and particular needs and concerns of the moment as defined by individuals and organized sectors of Puerto Rican society.

As the much heralded "fluidity" of the Puerto Rican racial scheme encounters the current emphasis in the United States on a "color blind" approach to resolving racial inequality, many have been left in a twilight zone of ambiguity, in search of some other possible source of cohesion. This need for an identity that encompasses and transcends the logic of previous and current social relations is especially acute among Puerto Ricans born and raised in the United States. The search for "roots" takes on even greater significance for these children of the Puerto Rican diaspora who, like the "little lost Taíno" quoted above, feel disconnected and undefined, seemingly presented with too many and too few identity choices. It is for these children of the Puerto Rican diaspora that the Taíno offers a respite, a safe haven from the complications of displaced colonial identity. The new Taíno movement is born of, and holds the greatest appeal for, those who seek relief from "the reproach and shame [they have] felt toward being Puerto Rican" in the metropole.[5]

Thus we find that the overwhelming majority of self-identified Taínos live in the United States. They are members of various recently formed organizations based in New York, New Jersey, and Florida which, in the past seven years or so, have effectively insinuated themselves into the national and international indigenous movements through a combination of old and new ideas and methods that both depend upon and reject official documentation and traditional discourse. The most striking feature of this reinterpretation of the Taíno past—and, more generally, of Puerto Rican history—is the insistence on indigenous survival against the Spanish onslaught and their continuing presence as a subjugated "nation."

This essay proposes to look at two crucial issues, sovereignty and authenticity, in the formulation of the new Taíno identity and within the context of Puerto Rico's colonial relationship to the United States. I begin with a brief discussion of how these same issues are played out among Native Americans in the United States. Not only is that experience crucial to situating the Taíno revival as a "New Age" expression of nativism, but it also poses the difficulties of identity claims based on natural rather than social criteria. The second section, an historical overview of the uses and abuses of the Taíno construct in Puerto Rico, is followed by a discussion of the development of a Taíno identity in the United States. The new Taínos flourish in the United States as a present-day reality on the basis of an anti-colonial discourse shared with North American Indians and they find inspiration in elements of Taíno-ness developed in Puerto Rico that respond to the island's own political subordination to the United States. At the same time, the new Taíno movement incorporates aspects specific to the United States and especially to the Puerto Rican diasporic experience. This contextualization of Taíno revivalism is followed by an analysis of the ideas expressed by self-identified Taínos, most notably those belonging to the Taíno Inter-tribal Council, based in New Jersey. One of the more prolific Taíno organizations, the Council makes active use of modern technology and their writings are readily accessible on the Internet. My intent is to demonstrate that identification as Taíno is intimately related to—and is, indeed, an expression of—the colonial relationship. As such, the decision to become Taíno is an inherently political act with serious political consequences.

Will the real Indian please stand up?

Until late in the 19th century in the United States, "the Indians are

104

coming" could only be voiced and understood as a White man's warning against the "savage" threat. It was a call to circle the wagons, protect the women and children, and prepare to defend the newly (and for the most part, illegally) acquired lands against the inferior barbarians who stood in the path of progress and civilization. The sympathetic and stereotypical figure of the Noble Savage, symbol of the pristine wilderness, a childlike guardian of nature, would only assume prominence in the popular imagination after the continent's indigenous peoples had been divested of their ancestral lands, almost exterminated through disease and warfare, and confined to reservations where they were directly and indirectly discouraged from following the very traditions that ostensibly made them "noble."

Largely ignored except by those federal offices charged with Indian "affairs," many Native Americans stepped forward in the late 1960s, joining other disenfranchised minority groups in the United States in their claims for social equality and justice. During that period of assertive rebellion, a militant Indian movement emerged which rejected the assimilationist policies of the federal government and demanded recognition of Indian nations as distinct, colonized entities with the right to self-governance and cultural autonomy. In other words, the struggle was defined by many as one of national liberation against colonial oppression. "The Indians are coming" again presented a threat, but this time within a social context that acknowledged, however grudgingly, the legitimacy of Native American grievances.

There were, of course, legal precedents for these claims. Until the 1920s the government of the United States negotiated with American Indians as it did with any foreign nation. In a time span of approximately 100 years, Congress ratified more than 350 treaties with various indigenous governments.[6] Fifty years of federal attempts to diminish Indian rights to self-governance (which began in earnest with passage of the Major Crimes Act in 1885) were consolidated when, in response to the growing corporate interest in extracting mineral deposits from Indian reservations, citizenship was unilaterally conferred in 1924.[7]

The past quarter century has brought significant changes in all our lives, not the least of which has been the very way we view our lives, who we are and where we came from. Inspired by the African-American movement to reclaim roots and assert pride in one's cultural heritage, other minorities have also searched and discovered the richness of their history and cultures. It is, of course, a continuing process of questioning old "truths" and challenging self-serving interpretations of the past—from whatever front—and the task is very far from over. But today we *should* know that the Indians "were coming" to retrieve what was, by all rights, theirs. From a progressive political perspective, the "threat" posed by this counter-narrative should be seen as a positive force, one that is potentially liberating.

Still, sometimes the newfound awareness of ancestral cultures has been put to questionable use, and it is at best a dubious sign of progress that today more people than ever before claim Native American ancestry. The invisible Noble Savage has seemingly been brought out of the closet with a vengeance, this time as both "New Age" symbol of spiritual harmony with the earth and as representative of one more of the multiple cultures that constitute the ethnic diversity of the United States. In 1960, for example, the United States Census Bureau reported a total of half a million American Indians; thirty years later, almost two million people identified as Indian, an increase that cannot be explained by immigration patterns or laws of natural reproduction.[8] One exasperated Native American educator and activist explained the problem as one of lack of "control."

> First there was this strict quantum blood thing, and it was enforced for more than one hundred years, over the strong objections of a lot of Indians. Then when things were sufficiently screwed up because of that, the feds suddenly reversed themselves completely, saying it's all a matter of self-identification. Almost anyone who wants to can just walk in and announce that he or she is Indian . . . and under the law, there's not a lot that Indians can do about it . . . . At that point, you really did have a lot of people showing up claiming that one of their ancestors, seven steps removed, had been some sort of "Cherokee princess. . . ." Hell, if all of that was real, there are more Cherokees in the world than there are Chinese.[9]

Clearly, the claim to the right of self-identification is not without problems, often bringing into play the very questions of authenticity it may have intended to resolve. In the United States, these issues of legitimacy are intimately tied to a well-documented 200-year history of continual conflict (expressed in those infamous words "The Indians are coming") and dispute over land and sovereignty rights. This is the case for the Navajos, Lakota, Cherokees, and dozens of other recognized Indian nations. Such is not the case, however, for the Ramapoughs along the New Jersey–New York border, who have been refused official acknowledgment, and until the 1970s, such was not the case for the Golden Hill Paugussetts or the Mashantucket Pequot Indians of Connecticut. (The Pequot have recently received international attention as the owners of the Foxwoods Casino, the country's most profitable gaming center, with annual gross earnings of over $800 million a year, double those of their competitors in Atlantic City and Las Vegas.) Federal recognition, however, does not necessarily mean a sustained cultural "authenticity." For the Pequot, official recognition and the gambling empire that has resulted means that they can now hire anthropologists to teach them how to be Pequot. As one tribal member put it, "We've picked up many of your western regalia here, costumes and bells, but that wasn't our people."[10]

"Our people," according to the Pequot, are those descended from a "full-blooded tribe member" no more than four generations removed. For the Pequot, self-identification has its limits and documented "blood quantum" is the final criterion for determining tribal membership. One need not "look" like an Indian—indeed, the Pequot are wrestling with serious problems of racism within their community since tribal members include people who, until very recently, identified, and were accepted, as White or Black.[11] Similarly, for the approximately 140 tribes currently seeking federal recognition, compliance with the seven "tests" demonstrating continuous existence since first contact with Europeans also demands individual documentation of indigenous descent. Thus, both the U.S. government and the respective tribes condition "Indian-ness" on the biological proof of origins. For most of the groups, such proof—depending as it does on documentation gathered by the very authorities historically intent on making the Indian disappear—is impossible to obtain.[12]

The extremely complex and confusing situation of the Native

American in the United States leaves wide open the possibility of claims to "Indian-ness" as long as it places no demands on the federal government or hinders corporate interests. Looked at from this perspective, self-identification as Indian in this country serves to diminish the legitimate claims of those who actually suffer the consequences of being Indian, while maintaining the illusion of liberal acceptance of difference. It becomes all the more problematic, when the United States narrative of the Indian is appropriated, adapted, and imposed onto other realities. This is the case in the Caribbean, where the appropriation of the North American "red man" includes the use of figurines and statues in Santería and Espiritísmo that serve as spiritual "guides" to the faithful.[13] The North American Indian motif is also prominently displayed in colorful carnival costumes throughout the Caribbean. In all instances, and even when linked to local indigenous history, the primary arbiter of what constitutes an Indian would appear to be Hollywood.

The "red man" stereotype takes on even greater significance wherever the numbers of *indios* are notable. Central and South America, which has never wanted its Indians except as historical artifact, has proved quite receptive to a narrative that rationalizes vanquishing the "savage" and dominating "nature's child." After all, *el indio* does not fit easily into the *mestizo* construct that emphasizes racial mixture as the national ideal and the best path toward Whiteness. If the "red man" construct of the United States is the "real" Indian, then Latin America does not have to contend with its indigenous peoples on their own terms. Similarly, for Latin Americans, the "real" Black people are those in Africa—or those who come from the United States, or the "islands," generally read as the English-speaking Caribbean—or those from somewhere else and thus "alien" to the nation. Again, a basic tenet of the *mestizo* construct is the disappearance of its parts. Accordingly, this literal and figurative "disappearance" of the *indio* and *negro* provides the necessary space in which to accommodate the "red" and "black" racial construct of the politically and economically dominant United States.

For Puerto Ricans, the (more) direct colonial relationship facilitates—and to a certain extent, encourages—the adoption and adaptation of these racial constructions. The effects of this relationship are evident on the island, where anthropologists and archeologists, guided by their North

American colleagues and similarly dependent on federal programs and funding, have created a "scientific" basis for the continued relevance of the Taíno for Puerto Rican national identity. It expresses itself, as well, in the United States, where Puerto Ricans search for a cohesive identity that accommodates the various narratives in all their diversity—the island racial triad, Spanish and United States anti-colonialism, Blackness, Whiteness, Latinidad—and yet, in the process, establishes their uniqueness and legitimacy as a people. Efforts at reconciling the national myths of Puerto Rico and the United States often result in a hodgepodge of conceptual contradictions.

The Basis for Becoming Taíno in Puerto Rico

Unlike the situation in the United States and in most of Latin America, the indigenous people of Puerto Rico, far from being a tangible presence, have been understood to be an extinct, yet important symbol of national identity. Indeed, before 1492, there were no "Taínos." When Christopher Columbus first landed on the northern coast of "Hispaniola," he promptly named the island in honor of his Spanish benefactors. Just as expeditiously he designated the indigenous people whom he encountered "Taínos" because he assumed that in greeting him with the word "taíno" they were naming themselves. In fact, they were offering assurances of their harmlessness (the word, the Spanish would soon learn, actually meant "noble" or "good"), and were trying to distinguish themselves from their more aggressive neighbors, the "Caribs," who inhabited the islands to the southeast.[14] The Taínos also made other distinctions among themselves, but the Spaniards considered these to be irrelevant, and except for certain contemporary scholars, these distinctions remain of little concern to anyone else. Today, they are all Taínos, and commonly considered the original inhabitants of most of the islands of the Caribbean.[15] Information on this homogeneously constructed Taíno society relies heavily on the incomplete Spanish chronicles and the archeological studies that have been carried out most intensely since the 1950s. The studies are also supplemented with ethnological research on contemporary indigenous peoples that are of questionable usefulness because at least 500 years separate the pre-Columbian Taínos from their modern Arawak cousins in the Guianas and Venezuela.

Paradoxically, it is to the Spanish conquerors, that is, to those responsible for their disappearance, that we owe the greatest debt regarding direct knowledge about the Taíno. The bulk of this paltry information concerns only the very earliest years of contact in Hispaniola (Haiti and Dominican Republic) and Puerto Rico since the Spaniards quickly lost interest in learning about the rapidly declining native populations of these and other islands and were instead focusing their attention on obtaining African laborers to replace them. The information they provided on language, religion, and social relations was scant, speculative, and clearly tainted by their own perspectives and biases. Estimates as to the number of Taínos present in Puerto Rico during the first contact with the Europeans, for example, range from as many as one million to as few as 16,000.[16] Later, in the 1530's, the Spaniards reported that 1,545 *indios* (which also included those taken from other islands), and 2,281 *Africanos* were serving 331 free citizens (which included free Blacks and Whites).[17] Even allowing for the island-based Spaniards' incentive to underestimate the Indian population in order to obtain more enslaved Africans, it was already apparent that the Taínos were becoming extinct, rapidly succumbing to disease, brutal working conditions, and widespread miscegenation.

In contrast to the approach taken more than one hundred years later by English colonists in what ultimately became the United States, the Spanish did not negotiate over issues of territory or autonomy with the indigenous populations of the Caribbean. Instead, the Indians were declared subjects of the Crown, which also obliged them to work for the Spaniards under the *encomienda* and *repartimiento* systems of labor. Indigenous resistance to Spanish authority, often in alliance with enslaved Africans, was quickly crushed.[18] Attempts at overthrowing Spanish domination included the very first documented active rebellion in Puerto Rico in 1514, in which two Taíno chiefs and their people joined Black *ladino* rebels in an unsuccessful bid for freedom.[19]

The "mixing" of peoples, which had preceded the coming of the Spanish,[20] would grow in scope and intensity as a predominantly male and Spanish power elite would assert its dominance over Indian and African women.[21] On the other hand, the barbarous conditions imposed on all enslaved Indians and Africans, and the shared intimacies of daily life encouraged collaborative efforts, from the most basic level of individual survival to the more extreme political formation represented by *marronage*. Sixteenth-century reports to the Spanish Crown often referred to the difficulties involved in controlling the "mestizos, mulattoes, negroes and indians, as well as poor whites" who fled into the hills and swamps to escape forced labor and other colonial impositions.[22] It would be in these "free zones," in the swamps as well as the hills, the coast as well as the mountains, and with other fugitives from Spanish rule, that the Taíno (and other indigenous peoples brought to the island by the Spanish) would find the conditions most suitable for practicing and sharing, and thus passing on, their cultures.[23] As the numerical majority and similarly oppressed group, Africans and their descendants would be the primary keepers of these traditions.

Although the *"indio"* classification would disappear completely from the census tallies by the late 18th century, it continued to be used as a descriptive term. In a caste society increasingly reluctant to acknowledge its African ancestry, Puerto Ricans would explain their dark skin as due to Taíno ancestry.[24] Other "national characteristics" would also be explained as the result of the Indian heritage; the goodness, docility, and hospitality that permitted their conquest by the Spanish would serve as well to explain the continuing subordination of Puerto Rico to a foreign power. This role would take on added resonance in the 1950s when, largely through the efforts of anthropologist Ricardo Alegría and a newly created governmental agency, the Institute of Puerto Rican Culture (ICP), the Taíno was resurrected as symbol of cultural independence. As part of a nationalist project that would counter the clearly assimilitionist path which the new "Commonwealth" status represented, the Taíno was rescued from the past in order to serve as a cultural savior for "Puerto Ricaness." The Taíno simultaneously distinguished Puerto Rico from the United States and bound the island to Latin America, both racially and culturally. The three "races" were represented as harmoniously intertwined and resulting in a people with no specific racial identity. As the original "root," the Indian established the legitimacy of island tenancy (the island was not taken from the Taínos because, as part of the collective "us," they continue to possess it); the Spanish conqueror was re-imagined as a purveyor of "high" culture and a civilizing agent, the cement that holds the nation together; and the African presence was depicted as both a disappearing minority and as evidence of the absence of racism.

The Institute of Puerto Rican Culture erected monuments to the Taíno in the form of statues, parks, and museums; research and instructional programs assured the intellectual and popular dissemination of Taíno culture and myth. Ironically, these programs received an additional boost during the late 1960s and early 1970s as a result of federal civil rights legislation that recognized Puerto Ricans as a racial minority and provided funding for ethnically specific cultural events. Representative of these programs is the annual National Indigenous Festival, begun in 1969. Held in Jayuya and organized by the town's ICP-affiliated Cultural Center, the festival attracts thousands of outsiders to an economically desperate area, where more than 75 percent of the population lives below the poverty level.[25] While the festival's site reaffirms the longstanding (and certainly oversimplified) portrayal of the mountains as the last refuge of the Taíno, and the *jíbaro* as the vessel of continuity with the past, the townspeople express little interest in what they perceive as a "ridiculous and contrived" affair that owes more to the machinations of anthropologists, archeologists, and partisan political agendas than to a legitimate indigenous survival.[26] This stance is consonant with the ICP's emphasis on the symbolic significance of the Taíno even as it puts into question the characterization of Jayuya as the "Taíno capital of Puerto Rico."

On the island, contemporary expressions of Taíno symbolism have been most apparent in cultural and commercial endeavors, the two often linked. During the 1970s, Puerto Ricans—many of them sporting fashionable Afros and dashikis—attended the increasingly popular cultural festivals held throughout the island and purchased items stamped with indigenous "fertility" symbols. T-shirts, key rings, belts, ashtrays, plaques and countless other utilitarian craft items were soon joined by corporate media campaigns that also played to an indigenous national romanticism. A major U.S. manufacturer of corn oil (Mazola) launched an "Herencia del indio" advertising campaign that included a sweepstakes, calendars, posters, and lavish, lengthy commercials shown to Puerto Rican television and movie theater audiences. This Hollywood version of the noble savage—tall, well-formed and bronzed Indians, with glistening bodies (another use for cooking oil?) gather the crop from the heavily laden corn stalks, place them into big, woven baskets, and carry them to their *bohios*, where the (beautiful) communal family prepares its meal in smiling fellowship—was enthusiastically received, and it was not unusual to find the posters, for example, prominently displayed in food and drinking establishments throughout the island. At one such place in Loiza, a town repeatedly promoted as *the* Black enclave on the island, a very dark-skinned bartender defensively responded to statements questioning the display of posters with Indian motifs by asserting: "After all, we're all part Taíno." More recently, a cartoonist has found indigenous inspiration for his comic strip "Turey, El Taíno," a character who wears only a loincloth and a feather in his rawhide sweatband and whose naiveté borders on idiocy.[27]

Today, souvenir shops display eclectic collections of "authentic" cultural artifacts in which paintings of muscular, warrior braves, sensual squaws, and tribal chiefs in full regalia vie for space amid religious paraphernalia ranging from crucifixes to seven-day candles to rock crystals. These are, however, isolated expressions of an indigenous identity that has traditionally been associated with anti-United States sentiments.[28] For the vast majority of Puerto Ricans, of whatever political persuasion, the Taíno is a quaint historical figure, having little to do with contemporary life. Puerto Ricans are understood to be "part Taíno"—as they are *part* Spanish and *part* African—but generally speaking, to call oneself a Taíno (or a Spaniard or an African) in Puerto Rico is to be subject to ridicule, albeit for a variety of reasons. Within a racial hierarchy primarily based on phenotype, rather than ancestry, one may *look* Indian but "*looking* Taíno is never equated with *being* Taíno."[29]

Significantly, though the Taíno remains a largely symbolic component of Puerto Rican national identity, the indigenous "part" has received considerably more attention than the more obvious African foundations and the continuing presence of their (Black) descendants. No museums or monuments exist that specifically celebrate Black contributions to the formation of Puerto Rican society on the scale dedicated to the Taíno, and even token attempts to do so—as in the battle over the naming of the island's premiere cultural arts center—have been summarily rejected.[30] While the past two decades have witnessed a greater receptivity to Puerto

Rico's African roots, it has most frequently been characterized by an historical distancing that locates Africans and their descendants within the chronological and social confines of slavery and *marronage*, and a colorful exoticism in which drums, masks, and undulating bodies continue to represent the essence of the island's Black cultural expression. The more recent *antillanismo* that links Puerto Rico to the rest of the Caribbean (a Caribbean that extends beyond Cuba and the Dominican Republic) and is notable for its counter-hegemonic approach, including the reclaiming of the island's African foundations, has still not managed to divest itself of this simplistic view, so that *lo africano* remains in the past and heavily laden with erotic and primitive signifiers.[31] This may explain both the content and the popularity of literary and musical expressions that with rare exceptions ignore the contemporary manifestations of "race" and racism in favor of rhetorical romanticism.[32] It is indicative of the continuing reluctance to fully engage its Blackness—as a legacy of Africa, as an integral part of its history, and as a living, active presence—that a nation which defines itself as "a blend" of races and cultures still approaches the national culture and *lo negro* as distinct, and almost mutually exclusive, phenomena (witness the usage, even among antiracist writers, of terms such as "Afropuertorriqueño"). The conditional nature of Black membership in the *gran familia puertorriqueña* persists in making problematic, and thus unattractive, individual identification as a Black person.

And yet, despite a traditional, official ideology that emphasizes the "racially mixed" character of Puerto Ricans, it has become increasingly clear to many that the elements that go into the mixture are not given the same value and that the degrees of mixture have always mattered. The public questioning of the oft-cited racial triad which privileges the Spaniard, idealizes the Taíno, and largely ignores (when not actually debasing) the African component can be viewed as an act of defiance. In fundamental ways, these new lines of inquiry reflect the growing consciousness among Puerto Ricans that the hispanophilia that has characterized most of the past century, and continues to be offered as a counter-narrative to U.S. cultural imperialism, is premised on the very same racist assumptions about the preferability, if not the actual superiority, of whiteness and the undesirability of blackness. The acknowledgment of the existence of racism among Puerto Ricans, as a legacy of both Spanish and North

114

American colonialism, recognizes as its *primary* victims not Puerto Ricans as a "mixed race" group, but, specifically, those who are identified as Black.[33] In this sense, "race matters" in today's Puerto Rico, and bears a striking similarity to the racial discourse in the United States where, despite a long multiracial historical experience, the essential categories continue to be Blackness and Whiteness.[34]

The Basis for Becoming Taíno in the United States

Almost half of all Puerto Ricans live outside the island, a demographic reality directly attributable to its colonial status. Puerto Ricans have been (im)migrating to the United States in significant numbers since the late nineteenth century, when the island was a colony of Spain and dissidents sought refuge from political persecution in New York. The volume steadily increased throughout the past century, spurred on by the social and economic instability that has characterized Puerto Rico since the U.S. invasion in 1898, with Congressional mandates (most notably, the unilateral conferral of US citizenship in 1917) and the implementation of an industrialization program (Operation Bootstrap) that depended on, and actively promoted, relocation to the industrial centers of the Northeast. By 1960, Puerto Ricans in New York, where the vast majority settled, numbered more than half a million, representing over 80 percent of the total "Hispanic" population; by 1980, the Puerto Rican communities throughout the city consisted of a generationally mixed population of approximately one million.[35]

The largest population of "people of color" after African Americans (most of whom had also recently made the trip North and with whom they shared many socio-economic indicators), Puerto Ricans in New York demonstrated a marked reluctance to be identified with their fellow travelers in racist oppression. Aware of the disdain in which African Americans were held by the dominant society and carrying, along with their dreams for a better life, the belief in the inferiority of Black people, many Puerto Ricans emphasized a cultural uniqueness that presumably transcended racial concerns. Although clearly perceived and treated as "non-white," Puerto Ricans tended to arm themselves with an island racial construct that set them apart from *los Americanos* —their *mestizaje*, the basis for neutrality in the bi-polar racial antagonism that epitomized U.S. society. And as they directly encountered the institutionalized racism of the United States, many Puerto Ricans could—and often did—hold themselves apart as being neither white nor black, neither oppressor nor oppressed.

This exceptionalist posture, however, was more difficult to sustain during the turbulent 1960s and early 1970s, when calls to take a stance against the status quo were invariably phrased in racial terms. As "people of color" Puerto Ricans shared many of the grievances regarding racial discrimination, and particularly for those Puerto Ricans who were of visible African descent, the Black Power movement held special meaning. The Vietnam War protests, with their clear anti-imperialist foundations, also resonated among Puerto Ricans aware of the impact of colonialism in their own lives. Puerto Ricans joined other racialized minorities in demands for political and economic measures that would alleviate the poverty and marginalization of the inner city ghettos that they shared with African Americans. Even concerns that seemed culturally specific to "foreigners" found their inspiration in the ideas and strategies of the African American community: it is within the framework of cultural affirmation first articulated by the Black Power Movement that Puerto Ricans and other racialized minorities demanded bilingual education for their children and curricula that included their own stories. Puerto Ricans in New York found common cause with African Americans, and just as it was common to find them living as neighbors, it was not unusual to find them allied in struggles around labor, health, and education issues.[36]

In New York City, where Puerto Ricans and African Americans comprised the vast majority of "non-Whites" until the 1980s, ample evidence exists of the political cooperation and cultural exchange that resulted from their physical proximity and common material reality.[37] Second- and third-generation Puerto Ricans grew up with African Americans, meeting in the schools and streets, on the stoops, in the *bodegas*, and at the dance halls. Puerto Ricans and African Americans created official and "honorary" families together,[38] as well as a wealth of cultural innovations, including boogaloo, latin jazz, and rap, that reflected and nourished both groups. Salsa, a creation of New York's Puerto Rican and Cuban musical commu-

116

nity, found inspiration in African and Black-derived rhythmic and lyrical forms, primarily because the vast majority of the musicians, like their audience, were themselves Black and poor.[39]

Ironically, these responses to the conditions that brought African Americans and Puerto Ricans together also functioned to put into question their "Puerto Ricaness." Especially for those on the island, "Nuyoricans" were betraying their national roots and losing their cultural essence. Unable to speak "proper" Spanish and ignorant of the history of the "motherland," Nuyoricans were also criticized for their failure to achieve economic success, for their poverty, unemployment, lack of educational attainment, moral laxity, and criminality (including prostitution and drug addiction). In short, the Nuyoricans were blamed for being victims of their experiences as colonized racial minorities. Negative depictions of Nuyoricans are still prevalent in the Puerto Rican media, and many of the social problems that plague the island are routinely attributed to the destructive influence of return migrants.[40]

Stateside Puerto Ricans are keenly aware of these derogatory stereotypes, and Nuyorican literature of the past three decades is rich with anguished recollections of the sense of rejection and alienation experienced during visits to the island. Attempts to reconcile the romanticized image of Puerto Rico gleaned from parents and grandparents and the reality of life in the "entrails of the monster" have ranged from acquiescence and accomodation to defensive hostility and outraged denunciation. The cultural nationalism of the 1970s and 1980s, with its emphasis on Afro-Taíno roots, offered Nuyoricans a counter-hegemonic narrative that attempted to accommodate the traditional Puerto Rican racial triad to the reality of racial discrimination experienced by the majority of Nuyoricans. And it served as a crucial link to the African American community, the undisputed political vanguard at the time, and to the righteous Native American struggle. The resonance that it held can be gauged by the proliferation of African and Indian names conferred on businesses, organizations, buildings, pets, and children—inoffensive cultural markers that simultaneously asserted national pride in one's origins.

Still, Puerto Ricans as a group have maintained a racial and cultural distance that has, especially since the 1980s, increasingly served to link them to other "Latinos." In racial and ethnic surveys, Puerto Ricans have consistently chosen to identify as "Puerto Rican," and when that option has not been offered, as anything other than "Black." In a recent population survey conducted by the U.S. Bureau of the Census, only 4 percent of Puerto Ricans self-identified as Black, overwhelmingly preferring a White (61 percent) or Other (35 percent) designation.[41] When additional categories were provided, most Puerto Ricans self-identified as "Hispanic" (77 percent) or "White" (17 percent), with very few opting for a Black (1.4 percent) racial identity or, as would be expected given the ideology of *mestizaje*, as "Multiracial" (2.5 percent).

A less formal survey of Puerto Ricans conducted on the Internet produced similar results. When asked about their racial self-identification, 66 percent of the respondents living in the United States selected "White" (of which 21 percent claimed to be "unmixed") and 6 percent chose "Black." Although an additional 19 percent identified as "dark-skinned," an astounding 6 percent of this group attributed their color to environmental factors, that is, "[b]ecause of [a] sun tan."[42] Responses to questions regarding ethnic ancestry, which permitted multiple answers, are consistent with earlier racial categorization in the minimization of African ancestry (21 percent) and the emphasis on Spanish ancestry (74 percent). More surprising is that only 8 percent of respondents checked off the "African, Spanish, Taíno" triad.

Whatever their methodological shortcomings, such surveys suggest the selective use of culture as a qualifier of "race" and in some instances as a substitute. While race, like class, is perceived as an unpalatable notion, an ugly and potentially divisive issue that threatens Puerto Rican unity, culture is presented as a valid and honorable expression of group solidarity, untainted, morally justified, and non-political. Puerto Rican culture, built on the foundation of the New World's three "races" is simultaneously presumed to be empty of race or, at the very least, capable of transcending its significance. In practical terms, however, Black people are understood to have (the problematic) "race," while Indians—like Whites—have "culture" and spirituality. In the current climate of "color blindness," it is culture that remains an acceptable line of demarcation and defense. However, an examination of the new Taíno movement provides abundant evidence of the political motivations and consequences of a claimed identity that ignores or distorts history in the service of a largely hypothesized "culture."

118

Coming Together

The United Confederation of Taíno People, established in 1998, consists of organizations concerned with the "preservation and protection of the culture, heritage and spiritual tradition of the Taíno people."[43] Of the nine groups participating in the Confederation, all but two are based in the United States.[44] The Confederation is the result of various attempts, begun in 1992, at "reconciliation and unification," suggesting that relations among Taínos have been strained, if not actually hostile.[45] Indeed, conflicts persist over the authenticity and representativeness of particular individuals and perspectives.[46]

Groups of so-called Taínos meet on a regular basis, and are active participants at regional, national, and international events organized by indigenous tribes, cultural institutions, and governmental agencies. A recent activity commemorating women's history month, co-sponsored by *Presencia Taína* and the Long Island Native American Task Force, was held at the Smithsonian Institute's National Museum of the American Indian.[47] As a complement to its major exhibition on pre-Columbian Taíno art and culture, El Museo del Barrio displayed photographs and videos of "present-day" Taínos, as well as an installation in wood, described by the artist as "a memorial . . . to the ancestors and in particular to my grandfather."[48] Periodically, the American Museum of Natural History in New York City has featured "traditional" Taíno crafts and storytelling workshops for children led by "Taíno" Bobby González. Peter Guanikeyu Torres, president of the Taíno Inter-Tribal Council, and other self-identifying Taínos also make regular appearances at educational and cultural institutions. The Bureau of the Census maintains contact with at least one Taíno organization, recently requesting a response to a survey aimed at helping the Bureau "make policy, product and communication decisions."[49]

The proliferation of Taíno organizations in the United States and the ready acceptance of some Puerto Ricans as legitimate Indians suggests that it is both viable and easier to become a Taíno in the United States than it is in Puerto Rico. In fact, references to the colonial relationship not only flavor the language and ideas, but the very reality itself offers the conditions and opportunities for this Taíno revivalist expression to manifest itself. This is clearly the case with the Taíno Inter-Tribal Council of New Jersey, the most vociferous and prolific enunciators of *Tainismo* among the organizational members of the Confederation.

Established in 1993 and incorporated in the state of New Jersey in 1995, the Taíno Inter-Tribal Council is headed by Chief Peter Guanikeyu Torres, the "highly revered Taíno Elder who is believed to be the great grandson of the late Taíno Chieftain of the district of Jatibonico, known as Orocobix"[50] (Torres himself is more assertive in making ancestral claims, consistently identifying himself as "the surviving blood Chief of the Jatibonuco Taíno tribe").[51] The stated goals of the organization include the international promotion of "our Taíno Native American values (be they moral, religious or artistic) that are the true traditional values of our Taíno ancestors."[52] Among their other objectives are the repatriation of ancestral bones, religious objects, and artifacts; and the protection of "our Mother Earth." To these ends the Council has launched a series of documentation efforts, including projects for the compilation of a dictionary of the Taíno language, the tracing of genealogy, and the establishment of a "national" library and museum—although it remains unclear just which "nation," Puerto Rico, Taíno, or the United States, is being referenced. As a people who "still do confront the forces of genocide, colonialism and oppression each and every day," the Council's members demand the recognition of their right to maintain their culture with "sovereignty in the United States and abroad in Puerto Rico."[53]

For obvious reasons, Torres and his followers flatly reject the "so-called 'Taíno Extinction' stories" of the Spanish colonial chroniclers and their successors, insisting on the survival of direct descendants of the "three to six million Taíno human beings" who had been "a self-constituted free and sover[e]ign indigenous Nation . . . as far back as 3,000 years before Don Cristobal Colon."[54] In fulfillment of a "prophesy," the Taínos, the "true landlords of our Mother Atabey," have again risen, determined "to govern themselves as a free nation."[55] Torres proposes that, just as his "brothers to the North are nothing but indigenous nations living within a US colonial nation," the Taíno are a distinct people, and doubly oppressed.

120

> The Taíno people are neither of Puerto Rican, Domini-
> can, Jamaican, Cuban nor of the present Floridian
> nationality. We are *a separate Native American nationality*
> *that has existed for centuries among the Caribbean nations*
> subject to Spanish, English and French European domi-
> nation.[56] (Emphasis mine)

Thus, the Taíno Inter-Tribal Council posits all Taínos as a colonized people, victims, first of the Europeans, and now, of the dominant "Creole" population of the Caribbean. In the case of Puerto Rico, the Taíno are presented as doubly oppressed, a (Taíno) nation within a (Puerto Rican "Creole") nation within a (United States) nation. Demands for sovereignty are ostensibly directed at both "colonizers," although only the United States is in any position to give it. Both the demands and the conditions that make it tenable are rooted in colonialism. It is within the context of United States domination that Puerto Ricans are compelled to leave the island, but it is here, in the metropole, that an Indian identity becomes attractive, and perhaps even necessary, and where it has the possibility of being recognized as legitimate. The improbability of achieving sovereignty is likewise a consequence of colonialism, first because the Spanish regime effectively wiped out the Taíno, and second because the United States has proved quite successful in dismissing considerably stronger claims— including those of the internationally recognized nation of Puerto Rico for its own sovereignty. It is nothing less than ironic that, out of the struggles to affirm a largely mythologized Puerto Rican national identity, one sees the emergence of another, greater myth of indigenous continuity and nationhood.

In similar fashion, Torres and his adherents accept and distort the tra-ditional racial triad and its ideology, and simultaneously embrace and reject racial essentialism. The Jatibonuco Taínos, for example, are described as a "mestizo people" and visitors to their Website are invited to experience the "warm Jibaro hospitality of their mountain village." But theirs is a *mestizo* where the African plays a minor role (if at all) and the Spaniard is usually a vital component, albeit vilified. The romantic image of the *jibaro* (exclusively and thus, erroneously), recognized as a marriage between Spaniards and Taínos, is portrayed as the essential carrier of

Taíno culture. When María Anani Jiménez, "a Taíno spiritual woman who listens to her people," reported on her 1996 trip to Puerto Rico, among the events she described were "performances of Jíbaro music and many other Taíno dances."[57] In a poem that resonates with pop culture allusions, Torres writes of Taíno resistance and survival as achieved thanks to the "machete in his hand," even though the machete was a weapon unknown to Caribbean indigenous peoples.[58]

Similar cultural attributions are made by another self-identified Taína who laments the passing of indigenous traditions, such as the roasting and grinding of coffee, or the making of cups from coconuts and the preparation of corn fritters ("tortitas de maíz"): none of these activities having been practiced by the Taínos. Coffee and coconut palm trees were introduced by the Spanish, and Taínos never developed the sophisticated corn processing techniques found among the Indians of Central and South America.[59] Other inaccurate cultural attributions include the origins of *arroz con gandules,* the island's national dish (*gandules* are an African contribution to the Caribbean diet); the celebration of *parrandas* and the Three Kings (Roman Catholic customs that arrive in Puerto Rico via Spain); the non-culturally specific practices of fishing and planting of food crops; and, of course, the essentialist cliché that Taínos have bequeathed us their altruism, generosity, and respect for nature.[60]

Nor is it unusual to find contradictory statements regarding the racial make-up of Taínos. In their electronic newsletter, for example, after denouncing "the Spanish government and its historians" for spreading (false) rumors about their demise ("the Taíno People were decimated by the Spanish, but *were never extinct*"), the Council concludes that "the Taíno Indians of today are mainly mestizo mixed blood Native Americans," but it also proclaims that "the Cachepuela family in Ciales, Puerto Rico, are full blood Taínos!"[61]

That the assertion of mixed ancestry is qualified by an insistence on purity signals the weakness in the racial triad construct. It permits, if not actually encourages, a claim to biological purity. The Cachepuela family is lauded not simply for being Taínos who, after all, "are mainly mestizo," but specifically for being "full blood" and, by implication, more authentic. And yet, it is on the grounds of *cultural* authenticity that Torres (who describes himself as "jincho"[62]) makes his own claim to Chiefdom. The

Taínos had a hierarchical social structure with a hereditary nobility, and Torres is the "great grandson" of the Cacique Orocobix. Presumably, Torres does not have to look like a Taíno because royal blood flows through his veins.

Genealogy—the documentation of one's "blood" ancestry—plays an important role in the work of the Jatibonuco Tribe. A Taíno Elders Documentation project proposes to record all available Taíno family genealogy and mountain culture, while the "National Directory List" and "Taíno Genealogy Project" count with support from individuals at governmental and cultural institutions, including the Genealogical Society of Ponce, federal and island archivists and anthropologists, and "a Taíno DNA researcher" at the University of Puerto Rico. The projects are intended to bring together the "many people of Taíno blood dispersed throughout the United States."[63] Coupled with Torres' own claims to noble ancestry, this genealogical emphasis suggests a quest for nobility and not just indigenous heritage—the latter a claim that all Puerto Ricans can presumably make. Genealogy has traditionally been the province of an elite that seeks hereditary justification for its dominance, and in this respect, the Inter-Tribal Council is promoting an elitist project. It is also a largely futile effort given the paucity of reliable records; most Puerto Ricans cannot trace their family lineage beyond the fourth generation and, as already noted, the *indio* classification ceased to appear on census tracts in 1802, and from any other public records a century earlier.

"Taíno Indigenous blood" is nonetheless stipulated as a basic requirement for full membership in the Council, although sympathizers willing to promote Taíno culture may be accepted as adopted members (*Guaitiaos*), i.e., honorary Taínos. Membership requires the initial submission of a letter explaining the reasons for wishing to join and four photographs "for Inter-Tribal membership picture ID review." If this "review" is passed, the Membership Committee determines whether the "applicant [is] of Taíno Native American blood." The Council charter does not discuss the criteria used by the Committee in the making of this determination, but the repeated references to "blood" and the high priority given to a genealogy that cannot be proved strongly favor those who "look" Taíno.

Visual representations of Taínos reinforce this notion of the importance of "looking" Taíno in order to *become* Taíno. This is loosely translated as "looking Indian," or so one gathers from the images disseminated on the Internet. On the Council's Website, for example, a youthful Torres is shown dressed in full ceremonial regalia, including a long feathered headdress atop his long flowing hair. A photograph of the middle-aged "Doña Varin," (a Spanish[!] title of respect) captures her sitting cross-legged on the ground as she works on a "traditional capa style bowl." There is also a smiling, long-haired, brown-skinned, round-faced young woman with feathers around her collar and in her sweatband. A caption reminiscent of 19th-century ethnographic studies introduces her as "A Taína Boricua Island Girl of Morovis from the Region of Jatibonico."[64]

What constitutes "looking Taíno" has doubtless been influenced by the Hollywood screen and the mass-produced iconography ostensibly depicting the American West. But it has also been gleaned from reports of the first Spanish conquerors, most notably Christopher Columbus (who described them as "young people, with handsome bodies and very fine faces..., large eyes and very pretty, and their skin the color of Canary Islanders or of sunburned peasants") and Bartolomé de Las Casas, who likened the Taíno wives of the Spanish colonists to Castilian women in their beauty and coloring.[65] Columbus and Las Casas, usually character-ized by Torres and his followers as "barbarians" and "foul liars," are apparently considered reliable sources regarding the physical attributes of the Taíno. They are frequently quoted in Council writings regarding the beauty and nobility of the Taíno, even as their other observations are held up to ridicule and condemnation. More tellingly, there is an uncritical acceptance of European notions of beauty, one that logically extends to how Africans and their descendants are viewed.

Everything would suggest that a "true" Taíno cannot be too dark and that, given the paramount importance assigned to hair texture, very dark-skinned, nappy-headed Puerto Ricans would have difficulty passing muster with the Inter-Tribal Council's membership committee. Indeed, the "Indian look" is intentionally cultivated so that when the new Taínos con-gregate, one is struck by the brown-ness of their skin and the straightness of their hair, the latter often the result of chemical relaxers. Those with lighter complexions are much less apologetic about their looks, suggesting that the greater scrutiny is reserved for darker "Taínos." The weight given to phenotype is certainly not lost on one writer to a Taíno discussion group. Seeking information regarding his "native roots," he asserts that his grandmother "was *pura* Taína because her features are typical of Taínos." It remains a mystery whether he is making the call based on the Spanish accounts of Castilian beauties or the Plains Indian stereotype that seems to prevail among self-identified Taínos. But fifty years ago, his grandmother would have been a "trigueña" (with all the lack of specificity that the term encompasses) in Puerto Rico, and thirty years ago she would have been "colored" in New York, with little question about her African "roots."

It can be argued that, by definition, Puerto Ricans as a *mestizo* people all qualify for Taíno membership, but there is a clear premium in looking the part, particularly given the absence of any other "proof." Almost by definition, the privileging of the Taíno comes at the expense of the African, as a contribution by one self-identified Taína to a discussion on Latino identity suggests. Responding to an earlier communication regarding the overwhelming African presence in the Americas, a Council member dismisses this as "rather Afro-centric" because she herself:

> has yet to find an African Peruvian, and as far as most PRs being African/European mix with a sprinkling of Native. . . . My guelita Juana is probably rolling over in her grave. . . . Not to say that African is not a significant race as a mixture in PR, but to say it is more significant than the Taíno to that racial mixture is not just uninformed, but absurd.[66]

"Guelita," the diminutive form of "grandmother," is apparently the writer's own claim to Taíno "blood"—an allusion that evokes the expression, *Y tu agüela, ¿'ónde ejtá?*, traditionally used to refer to Puerto Rican reluctance to acknowledge African ancestry. In her rejection of the African as a significant presence in Peru (and by implication the rest of South America) she not only demonstrates her ignorance about the peopling of the Americas, she also specifically pits the African against the Taíno, linking Puerto Rico to the *indigenous* Native American in Latin America. Again, the Taíno supplants the African in the racial identity of the Puerto Rican and places the new Taíno firmly within the old racist paradigms.

125

Conclusion

The new Taíno movement is clearly a phenomenon of the 1990s, a product of the cumulative effects of colonialism, migration, and racism—and of the identity politics that have characterized the past decade. It responds to a very real need for a positive identity and social purpose, one that is not plagued by the largely negative image associated with being Puerto Rican in the United States. The nostalgia for an idyllic homeland is a recurring theme among those who identify as Taíno and with this yearning for the past, comes its correlate: a rejection of what Puerto Rico has become, or, perhaps more to the point, an insistence that it return to what it never was.

This desire for something "better" is inextricably tied to the diasporic experience. In her study of Taíno cultural retentions, for example, Nilsa Olivero confesses, "I long for the island of Puerto Rico. Sometimes I wonder what it would have been like to grow up in a more serene environment than in New York City." One of Olivera's respondents expresses similar dissatisfaction with the experience of growing up a racialized minority in New York:

> I never liked the tone and manner in which people who are not from the culture refer to the group Puerto Rican; "look at that Puerto Rican" or "look at that Boricua," it is the tone they would use. The New York Puerto Rican is different from the Puerto Rican born and raised in Puerto Rico. The morals and beliefs are different. You see they are young and learn bad habits in today's way. They learn things moral that are different . . . too liberal, too much freedom.[67]

The reality of discrimination and poverty is contrasted with the myth of peace and harmony which Taíno traditions represent and indeed, for some, the latter erases the significance of the former.

But the claim to being Taíno is also a claim on the island of Puerto Rico where the Nuyorican is viewed as inauthentically Puerto Rican. A woman whose parents encouraged her to assimilate into the dominant United States culture and whose cousins in Puerto Rico subjected her to

126

"royal snubbing" reports that "[a]s Taíno I am beginning to feel closer to the term [Borinqueña] because it focuses on the spiritual aspect of what the island stands for, the green beauty. Forget the politics and the high unemployment rate on the island . . . there is the essence of the island that you cannot deny. I am Borinqueña and I am Taíno."[68] Implicit is the assertion of authenticity, indeed of doing the islanders one better: as a Taíno one is presumably more rooted in the land, less tainted by contemporary mores and values, and thus a more legitimate landlord for Borikén.

Beyond the wholesale adoption of the more recent manifestations of the Red Man stereotype, Taíno revivalism exhibits a largely uncritical acceptance of the stereotypes that pervade the dominant understanding of indigenous peoples. In the absence of "a living, tribally based community" the self-proclaimed Taínos can only "identify with and organize or form themselves around metaphors that now identify indianess in the dominant society."[69] While not unique to the Taíno revival (as noted earlier, the Pequots and other federally recognized tribes have also "picked up" symbols of "Indianness" in their search for authenticity), expressions of Indianness also encompass the island constructs. Thus the new Taíno movement depends on two fictions to develop and promote a third: the existence of a subjugated Taíno nation.

In the final analysis, one's racial or ethnic identity is an individual matter, but it is also always political. Culture does not operate in a vacuum. In a racist society, past and present understandings of race condition the choices we make regarding identity—including the rejection of any racial identity at all. Puerto Ricans have been racially discriminated against, not because of their Taíno ancestry, but because of their African ancestry. Both on the island and in the United States, negative stereotypes abound about Black people, touching on every aspect of their physical and psychic being. In comparison, the self-proclaimed Taínos are treated gently— merely seen as naïve. Under these circumstances, Taíno identity is a relatively safe place. It also permits an easier entry into "Latinidad"—a territory that has only grudgingly welcomed Puerto Ricans in the past.

By jumping on the Indian bandwagon, the so-called Taínos take their cue from the dozens of Indian nations that have sought, sometimes with stupendous success (as in the case of Pequot), official recognition from the U.S. government. The Taínos, however, make identical claims without any historical foundation. These claims are based on the well-known and well-deserved distrust of the federal government, and on the general ignorance about the history and culture of Puerto Rico. The liturgy regarding the racial mixture of Puerto Ricans, and the concomitant reification of "pure races," makes it feasible to believe that Taínos are not truly extinct but simply denied recognition by a government intent on robbing Indians, and other racialized minorities, of their rights.

The decision to identify as Taíno cannot be divorced from material reality. Our choices are always circumscribed by the options open to us, and the options in turn are complicated by what is attributed to them. The *mestizaje* construct would seem to offer Puerto Ricans the choice of being Black, White, Red, or all of the above. But Blackness, Whiteness, and Redness each carry ideological baggage, and as a group, Puerto Ricans, demonstrating a clear understanding of the hierarchy of this racial structure, consistently opt away from Black racial identity. As Black identity itself becomes ever more complicated, choosing to identify as other than Black also becomes an increasingly acceptable option. Whiteness and Blackness are both rejected in favor of an exotic and unthreatening "middle ground" that ultimately calls on biology to buttress claims of spiritual identity.

But while the new Taíno movement offers an alternative that may seem culturally and racially comforting, providing a safe haven from the identity conundrum of displacement that especially plagues the children of immigrants, it remains an identity of reaction and conservatism. Rather than posing a challenge to the racial and colonial constraints on Puerto Rican identity, the Taíno revival movement is the latest product of those boundaries, dependent upon and nourished by ideologies of hierarchy. Far from serving as a tribute to the memory of Puerto Rico's indigenous peoples, today's self-professed Taínos—with their loincloths and feathers and calls for territorial sovereignty—add but one more insult to the many offenses already perpetrated in the name of national identity. The Taínos may well be coming, but the question remains: just where do they think they are going?

Notes

1. Rebekkah B. Rodríguez, Institute for Puerto Rican Policy, E-mail Forum, November 4, 1997.

2. The growing Black and Indian consciousness movements throughout Latin America have had to wrestle precisely with the invisibility of its constituency because the *mestizaje* construct does not recognize the parts of the idealized whole in any but the most abstract of terms. The peasant revolt in the Mexican state of Chiapas is but one example of the struggle of Indians and Blacks in Latin America for recognition as part of a nation and speaks to the centuries of marginalization which make their communities among the poorest in the hemisphere. Still, it is indicative of the greater legitimacy accorded indigenous communities that Black communities in Latin America have been directing their efforts at receiving official recognition as "indigenous regions," a designation that entitles them to a certain degree of territorial and political autonomy. Colombia and Mexico have already formally recognized Black communities as Black ethnic enclaves. Similar requests have been put forth in Peru, Ecuador and Central America.

3. For a discussion of the Mexican policies see Alan Knight, "Racism, Revolution and Indigenismo, Mexico 1910–1940," in Richard Graham, ed. *The Idea of Race in Latin America, 1870–1940* (Austin: University of Texas Press, 1997).

4. In general, the premise is that *indios* had and continue to have their own culture(s), while *negros*, as descendants of African slaves "lost" their cultures and acquired that of their European masters. This perspective also shaped U.S. policies towards Native and African Americans.

5. Op. cit., Rodríguez.

6. Rebecca L. Robbins, "Self-Determination and Subordination: The Past, Present and Future of American Indian Governance," in M. Annette Jaimes, *The State of Native America: Genocide, Colonization and Resistance*, (Boston: South End Press, 1992), p. 89.

7. Note that this occurred seven years *after* the people of Puerto Rico were made U.S. citizens, again suggesting the recognition of the relatively greater political autonomy of indigenous groups in the United States.

8. At the time of the Spanish conquest, it is estimated that approximately 15 million people lived in North America, of which 12 million resided in what is today the United States. The first recorded smallpox pandemic (1520–24) reduced the North American population by as much as 75 percent. By the

129

time the Indian Wars officially ended in 1890 the federal government determined that 248,253 identifiable Indians had survived. See Lenore A. Stiffarm with Paul Lane, Jr., "The Demography of Native North America: A question of American Indian Survival," in M. Annette Jaimes, ed., *The State of Native America: Genocide, Colonization, and Resistance* (Boston, Mass.: South End Press, 1992), pp. 23–53.

9. Statement by Lorelei Decora Means on radio station KILI, Poupine, South Dakota, October 12, 1986, as quoted in M. Annette Jaimes, "Federal Indian Identification Policy: A Usurpation of Indigenous Sovereignty in North America," in ibid, p. 130.

10. Attributed to Alan Pearson Jr., in Kirk Johnson, "Tribe's Promised Land is Rich but Uneasy," *The New York Times*, February 20, 1995, p. A1.

11. Among the newly united Pequots are the Cristensens, a family of White Mormons from Utah who are now forced to deal not only with Black Pequot relatives but with their own probable African ancestry. One young daughter dreamed that she had "turned black," presumably a traumatic experience.

12. The Ramapough (for centuries, popularly known as "Jackson Whites") have been refused recognition by the federal government which claims that the 3,000-member community is actually descended from 17th-century Dutch and African settlers.

13. According to Jimmie Durham, founding Director of the International Treaty Council, the world's first United Nations consultative Non-Governmental Organization, this is also the case in Latin America, where "the U.S. narrative has 'won' over those of Latin America" and informs its understanding of Indian-ness. A resident of Mexico for a number of years, Durham concludes that "[t]he mythical Plains Indians of the United States has become the archetype for 'Indian-ness,' has become the 'Red Indian' even for the indigenous peoples of Latin America." See Jimmie Durham, "Cowboys and . . . Notes on Art, Literature and American Indians in the Modern American Mind," in Jaimes, op. cit., p. 430.

14. "Caribs" was the designation given to "unfriendly" Indians. The Caribs, who resisted the Spanish—and later, other European—invasions, were depicted as hostile cannibals. Jalil Sued Badillo (*Los Caribes, realidad o fabula: ensayos de rectificación histórica*, Río Piedras: Editorial Antillana, 1978) has argued that the Spanish exaggerated the aggressiveness of the Caribs in order to rationalize their enslavement. Interestingly, it was to the allegedly vicious Caribs that the Spanish paid homage, naming the entire region after them, and not after the more hospitable Taínos.

15. According to Irving Rouse, and others, the West Indies were originally inhabited by the "Casimiroid" and "Ortoiroid," who succumbed to the "Saladoids" (ca. 200 B.C.) and their descendants, the "Ostionoids" (ca. 500 A.D.). The people who met Columbus were descendants of this latter group, with their emergence as a distinct cultural entity dated at 1200 A.D. "Taínos" identified themselves according to their island homes, i.e., Puerto Rico was "Borikén" and its inhabitants were "people of Borikén." There were also linguistic and other cultural differences among the "Taínos," reflected in their modern classification by scholars as "classic," "Western," and "Eastern" Taínos. For detailed discussion of the archeological and ethnohistorical evidence and abundant speculation on the Taíno, see Irving Rouse, *The Taínos: Rise and Decline of the People Who Greeted Columbus* (New Haven: Yale University Press, 1992).

16. Francisco Moscoso, *Tribu y clases en el Caribe Antiguo* (San Pedro de Macoris, República Dominicana: Ediciones de la Universidad Central del Este, 1986), p. 408.

17. Jalil Sued Badillo and Angel López Cantos, *Puerto Rico Negro* (Río Piedras, Puerto Rico: Editorial Cultural, 1986), p. 85.

18. Ibid., p. 69, and Rouse, p. 158. Resistance to Spanish authority included armed struggle, as well as escape and suicide.

19. Sued Badillo and López Cantos, pp. 175–189.

20. The Taíno of Puerto Rico maintained regular friendly contact with the people of Hispaniola, Cuba and Jamaica and conflictive relations with those to the southeast. The latter, designated "Caribs," who also included people classified as "Taíno," regularly raided island villages and kidnapped women. See Rouse, pp. 21–23.

21. It was standard practice for the Spaniards to distribute land, labor and women among themselves. In a letter dated 1493, a Spanish nobleman, Michele de Cuneo, boasted to a friend of his successful rape of "a very beautiful Carib woman" given him by Columbus. Cited in Antonia I. Castañeda, "History and the Politics of Violence Against Women," in Carla Trujillo, ed., *Living Chicana Theory* (Berkeley: Third Woman Press, 1998), p. 313.

22. In 1551, in an apparent effort to sever relations between Blacks and Indians, a law was passed making it illegal for Blacks to own or otherwise use the services of Indians. Sued Badillo, op cit., pp. 38–40.

23. Some of these peoples probably ended up in Puerto Rico since the Spanish relocated Indians from other islands and the mainland to meet immediate labor needs. During the earliest years of the conquest, thousands of Indians

from the islands of Hispañiola and Puerto Rico were also shipped to Europe and Africa. According to Forbes, "at least 3,000 Americans are known to have been shipped to Europe between 1493 and 1501, with the likely total being possibly double that." See Jack D. Forbes, *Africans and Native Americans: The Language of Race and the Evolution of Red-Black Peoples* (Chicago: University of Illinois, 1993), pp. 21–25.

24. The preference for Indian identification was further stimulated by economic considerations. In the 1770s, probably in an attempt by farmers to evade taxes from which indigenous people were, by definition, exempt, we find a number of people counted as *indios*. The last census in which *indios* are enumerated is that of 1778; the island's 2,300 "indios" *all* resided in the hilly, decidedly non-mountainous, southwestern town of San Germán. In the following years "indios" were counted as "pardos," i.e., mulattoes. See Fernándo Picó, *Historia General de Puerto Rico* (Río Piedras, Puerto Rico: Ediciones Huracán, 1988), p. 57. My thanks to Gabriel Haslip-Viera for bringing this to my attention.

25. Arlene Dávila, *Sponsored Identities: Cultural Politics in Puerto Rico* (Philadelphia: Temple University Press, 1997), pp. 222–223.

26. Ibid., p. 221. Probably the best known critic of the jibaro mystique is José Luis González who, in his controversial essay, *País de los cuatro pisos* (Río Piedras, Puerto Rico: Ediciones Huracán, 1980), accuses the island elite of elevating the mountain dwellers in an attempt at denying the African contribution to Puerto Rican cultural identity. For an English version of the essay see "The Four-Storeyed (*sic*) House: Africans in the Forging of Puerto Rico's National Identity," in Darién Davis, ed. *Slavery and Beyond: The African Impact on Latin America and the Caribbean* (Wilmington, Deleware: Scholarly Resources Inc., 1995).

27. Ricardo Alvarez-Rivón's cartoon, "Turey, El Taíno," appears in *El Nuevo Día,* one of the island's leading newspapers.

28. The perception of the Taíno as an ideological tool of the *independentistas* has waned somewhat as even the pro-Statehood forces have voiced support for archeological preservation efforts. Federal legislation and funds have resulted in the halting of construction projects when sites have been identified as containing Indian remains. These work stoppages have received broad coverage in the news media and appear to be creating a Taíno consciousness largely absent before.

29. Dávila, p. 228. Notwithstanding this *mestizo* construct, one's appearance remains of tantamount importance when it comes to the assigning of racial

identity. While there is some flexibility regarding skin color, candidates for the title of "Indigenous Queen," a contest held during the National Indigenous Festival, must have straight dark hair. This is only partly consistent with the traditional use of the descriptive term "indio/a" which refers to a dark-skinned individual with "good hair." Although chemical relaxers today make straight hair a readily available option, other considerations (facial features) take on greater significance.

30. For a discussion of the 1988 debate over the naming of the arts center see "Cortijo's Revenge; New Mappings of Puerto Rican Culture," in Juan Flores, *Divided Borders: Essays on Puerto Rican Identity* (Houston, Texas: Arte Público Press, 1993).

31. For an assessment of historical and cultural engagements with "Blackness" on the island, see Juan Giusti, "AfroPuerto Rican Cultural Studies: Beyond *cultura negroide* and *antillanismo*," in *CENTRO*, special issue on Race and Identity, vol. nos. 1 & 2 (New York: Centro de Estudios Puertorriqueños, Hunter College, 1996).

32. One such exception is Ruben Blades' salsa tune "Ligia Elena," which describes the love affair between a "White" upper-class girl and a "Black" (presumably poor) trumpet player and the distraught reaction of the girl's mother. The delicate subject is handled with heavy-handed humor, thus softening its possible impact.

33. Most notable among the activities marking the 100th anniversary of the United States colonization of Puerto Rico was the recently organized "Race and the Construction of Puerto Rican Identity: New Paradigms on Race, Identity and Power," a conference held in both New York City (April 22–24, 1998) and San Juan (April 29–May 1, 1998).

34. This is not intended to deny the differences in how Blackness and Whiteness have been (and continue to be) perceived and defined in various parts of the Americas, but rather to suggest that a consistent thread tying together all "New World" racial history is the polarity of the European and African.

35. Gabriel Haslip-Viera and Sherri L. Baver (eds.), *Latinos in New York: Communities in Transition* (Notre Dame: University of Notre Dame Press, 1996), pp. 14–15.

36. During the late 1960s and 1970s, many Puerto Rican youth were drawn to the Black Panther Party, and African Americans were members of the Puerto Rican Young Lords Party (YLP). In fact for some Puerto Ricans it was a toss-up whether to join the Black Panthers or the Young Lords. Pablo

"Yoruba" Guzmán and Felipe Luciano, two of the better known leaders of the YLP were originally attracted to the Black Panther Party, and Denise Oliver, an African American, was a member of the Central Committee of the Young Lords.

37. While most evident since the 1960s, when the children of the massive post-WW II immigration to New York City had come of age, political and cultural collaboration can be traced to the turn of the century. Bibliophile and lay historian Arturo Alfonso Schomburg (1874–1938) is the best-known Puerto Rican to make common cause with African Americans, but he was certainly not alone in recognizing that his own liberation was inextricably tied to that of African Americans in the United States. Through the decades there have been countlesss Puerto Ricans, some well known but most lost to the historical record, who have established working and personal relationships with African Americans that have resulted in some of the most exciting political and cultural creations of this century.

38. New York Congressman Charles Rangel, whose father was Puerto Rican and mother African American, and Councilman Adam Clayton Powell IV, son of the renowned Congressman and pastor of Harlem's Abyssinian Baptist Church and a Puerto Rican mother, are only two of the better known products of the more "intimate" relationship(s) between African American and Puerto Rican.

39. "In Puerto Rico music as a career choice was most commonly the province of black and *mulato* members of the working class." Ruth Glasser, *My Music is My Flag: Puerto Rican Musicians and Their New York Communities, 1917–1940* (Berkeley: University of California Press, 1995), p. 58.

40. For example, anti-drug public service announcements routinely depict the "dealer" as a Spanglish-speaking, dark-skinned youth: a clear reference to Puerto Ricans from the United States.

41. Figures cited in Tanya K. Hernández, "Over the Rainbow: Puerto Ricans and the 'Multiracial' Category in the Year 2000 Census," in *Crítica: A Journal of Puerto Rican Policy and Politics* no. 27 (August 1996), p 6.

42. The 281 respondents were overwhelmingly young (average age, 34 years), U.S. residents (65 percent) and male (64 percent), with professional or college degrees (73 percent). The racial self-identification question included ten options: White Mixed European/Non-European; White Mixed European; White Not Mixed; Dark Skinned Because of Sun Tan; Dark Skinned Mixed European Heritage; Dark Skinned Mixed European/Non-European; Black Mixed African/Non-European/European Heritage; Black Mixed African/

European Heritage; Black Not Mixed; Other. The authors' biases can also be gauged by their introductory remarks, which emphasize the Europeanization of Puerto Rico throughout the 19th and 20th century, making the island's people, in effect, predominantly "White." Shane Aaron Heiser and Juan Rodríguez-Vélez, "Just Wondering . . . A Puerto Rican Survey," Online posting, February 14, 1998, <http://www.execpc.com/~sh6i/index.htm>.

43. *La Voz del Pueblo Taíno*, Official Newsletter of the United Confederation of Taíno People—United States Chapter, vol. 1, Issue 1 (January 1998), p 1. (In this and subsequent quotes, orthographic marks have been added but spelling—including capitalization—are reproduced as in original).

44. The seven U.S.-based organizations are Maisiti Yucayeque Taíno, Taíno Intertribal Council of New Jersey, Presencia Taína, Baramaya, Taíno Tribal Council of Jatibonuco—New Jersey, Caney Spiritual Circle, and Cacibajagua. Also participating in the Confederation are Fundación Social Luz Cósmica Fraternalista Taína from Quisqueya (Dominican Republic) and El Consejo General de Taínos Borincanos from Puerto Rico. The Taíno Timucua Tribe of Florida maintains a web page on the Internet which is sponsored by the Jatibonuco tribe.

45. One of the first Taíno groups, "La Asociación Indigena Taína," split into three smaller groups in the early 1990s, including one which is now defunct and another (Taíno Nation) which recouped after undergoing a period of internal conflict.

46. In a letter (January 12, 1998) to El Museo del Barrio, Roger Hernández (aka Roger Atahuibacex) of *Presencia Taína* expressed his strong *"objection* to the detrimental special attention and favoritism [he] interpreted was focused unnecessarily on René Marcano and his followers" (emphasis his).

47. "The First Annual Native American Conference Celebrating and Honoring the Voice of Mother Earth," consisting of "songs, traditional drumming, poetry and [a] discussion panel" took place on March 28, 1998.

48. The two contemporary exhibits, *The Taíno Legacy* ("examining the persistence of Taíno culture in the contemporary Caribbean and its diaspora") and *Coaybay: Site of the Afterlife*, by artist and storyteller Jorge Crespo, were on display through January 11, 1998. El Museo del Barrio did not extend the viewing dates as it did for the principal exhibit, *Taíno: Pre-Columbian Art and Culture from the Caribbean*.

49. E-mail correspondence to the Taíno Inter-Tribal Council from Joanne C. Dickerson, Marketing Services Office, Washington, D.C.: Bureau of the Census, October 23, 1997.

50. "The Taíno Land Review" (*La Revista de la Indierra Taína*), official news-letter of the Taíno Inter-Tribal Council, April 1996, available at <http://www.hartford-hwp.com/taino/>. Born in Orocovis, the 46-year-old "relentless warrior" Peter Torres claims to have entered "the struggle for Taíno indigenous freedom" at the age of 14. His numerous siblings do not identify as Taíno (personal communication, March 1, 1998).

51. Web page for the Taíno Council of Jatibonicu <www.algorithms.com/users/torres/jatiboni.html>.

52. Taíno Inter-Tribal Council Charter, Adopted June 23, 1995, Amended May 16, 1996, Millville, New Jersey, <www.hartford-hwp.com/taino/docs/charter.html>.

53. Ibid, p. 3.

54. Chief Peter Guanikeyu Torres, "The historical roots of a Nation," <www.hartford-hwp.com/taino/docs/Tnation.html>. And yet, a book of poems by Torres bears the title *The Book of 8 Million Tears*.

55. The Council asserts original property rights over the Caribbean and parts of Florida. The Jatibonuco define their "village" as encompassing the Puerto Rican towns of Orocovis, Barranquitas, Morovis and Aibonito.

56. Taíno Inter-Tribal Council Charter, p. 3.

57. María Anani Jiménez, "Going Home," *La Revista de la Indierra Taína*, issue no. 2 (1997).

58. "LOOK in the TUREY? UP In the blue sky! It's a SCREAMING Eagle! It's a Red Tailed Guaraguao! It's a Jet plane with TALONS! No it's a PROUD WARRIOR Man!. . . MEMORIES of Our Sacred Cacique OROCOBIX, with a tear drop in his Left EYE! Would have even made Humble Chief Joseph cry!" in Chief Peter Guanikeyu Torres, "The Proud Taíno Warrior Man," excerpted from *The Book of 8 Million Tears* by Glenn Walker, Oct 28, 1997 <www.indigenouspeoples literature>. The "tear drop" appears to be a reference to Iron Eyes Cody, an actor in dozens of Hollywood westerns who, since the early 1970s, appeared in a well-known anti-littering television ad. Though he claimed to be Cherokee and Cree from the Oklahoma Territory, a 1992 investigative report by a New Orleans newspaper revealed that Cody was actually a second-generation Italian-American born in Louisiana. See *The New York Times*, January 5, 1999, p.A15. For an earlier charge of being an "imposter," see comment by Ted Jojola of the University of New Mexico on Nativenet <http://nativenet.uthscsa.edu/archive/nl/9202/0140.html>.

59. Nilsa Olivera, "Discovering Indigenous Characteristics Across Time and Space: The Taíno Woman" (Ph.D. dissertation, The Union Institute Graduate School, 1996). For a similar approach, see Toni Ann Ramos, "Maintenance of Taíno Traditions within Puerto Rican Culture" (Master's thesis, University of Arizona, 1995).

60. See Olivero, pp. 114, 119, 186; and Ramos.

61. Wilfredo Alvarado, "The HummingBird BBS Updates," *La Revista de la Indierra Taína*, issue no. 1, 1996.

62. Personal communication, March 1, 1998. "Jincho," one of the more common, but never offical, racial signifiers used among Puerto Ricans, refers to a paleness that borders on sickliness.

63. Taíno Inter-Tribal Council Charter, p. 3.

64. Web page for the Taíno Council of Jatibonicu <www.algorithms.com/users/torres/jatiboni.html>.

65. Cited by José Pedreira on website, "El Bohio Mio," <hudson.idt.net/~pedrei19/taíno1.html>.

66. Valerie Nana Turey Vargas Stehney, in Internet Archives: Tour Question on Latino Identity, June 27, 1997, <www.hartford-hwp.com/taíno/index.html>.

67. Olivero, p. 108.

68. Ibid.

69. In his discussion of Indian identity, Nicholas Peroff explains that "[m]ost people in American society know little or nothing about Indians or Indianess; however they may be familiar with many expressions of indianess" and thus depend on stereotypical metaphors such as "indianess as harmony with nature," "indianess as tourist attraction," and "indianess as historical artifact." The pervasiveness of this approach to indigenous peoples is captured in the following capsule: "All Indian tribes perceived their land as sacred territory from which they never moved for thousands of years, and which they worshipfully personified as Mother Earth, and upon which they lived in profound harmony; that to the Indian, all creatures, all things, all thoughts, and all natural phenomena were pervasively infused with the sacred; and that, in defiance of the laws that govern cultural change everywhere else in the world, the beliefs of the primeval Indians remain indelibly and irreversibly imprinted in the souls of their present day decendants, having been passed down for endless generations unaltered by contact with the outside world, as if Native

Americans alone among all the world's peoples existed utterly outside the flow of history." Cited by Nicholas C. Peroff, "Indian Identity," in Juan L. Gonzales, Jr., ed., *Racial and Ethnic Groups in America: A Collection of Readings* (Dubuque, Iowa: Kendall/Hunt Publishing Company, 1998), p. 247, citing Bordewich, F. *Killing the White Man's Indian: Reinventing Native Americans at the End of the Twentieth Century* (New York: Doubleday, 1996), pp. 210–211.

6.

ROBERTO MUCARO BORRERO

"Rethinking Taíno: A Taíno Perspective"

On February 28, 1998, I attended a symposium entitled "Rethinking Taíno: The Cultural Politics of the Use of their Legacy and Imagery," which took place at El Museo del Barrio in New York City in conjunction with the exhibit "Taíno: Pre-Columbian Art and Culture from the Caribbean." The objective of the panel was to explore the historical role of the Taíno as a symbol of national identity and its continued use as an important political and cultural symbol for the contemporary Caribbean. Panelists included Dr. Arlene Dávila, Syracuse University; Dr. Jorge Duany, Universidad de Puerto Rico; Dr. Peter Roberts, University of the West Indies at Cave Hill; and Ms. Miriam Jiménez Román, an independent scholar. Although I was not a panelist, I attended this symposium as a concerned person of Taíno descent, a representative of a Taíno organization, and a contributor to the Taíno Legacy portion of the exhibition.

The following review is an expanded and revised version of an article that was published in *La Voz del Pueblo Taíno*,[1] the official newsletter of the United Confederation of Taíno People. My main objective in writing this review/response is not only to offer an alternative to the scholarly perspectives presented at this symposium but also to expand the dialogue on the subjects of race, identity, and education. These are issues that directly concern Latin American and Indigenous Peoples and should be continuously revisited. It is important to note that the presentations given by the panelists were taken directly from essays that they had written specifically for this symposium. With the exception of the paper that was presented by Dr. Arlene Dávila, the complete essays were unavailable for public review. My observations and opinions, therefore, reflect only what transpired at El Museo del Barrio on the day of the symposium. I was also fortunate to review videotape of the proceedings that was generously made available to me by War Party Productions. Although incomplete, this video complemented the notes that I had taken during and after the presentation.

Ms. Fatima Bercht, the co
curator of the exhibition: "Taíno: Pre-Columbian Art and Culture from the Caribbean," made the opening statements. Ms. Bercht acknowledged the awareness of El Museo del Barrio for the growing number of persons asserting Taíno identity throughout the Caribbean and the United States. She explained that the panel would present some aspects of this "phenomenon" that she termed the "Taíno Legacy." After Ms. Bercht thanked the corporate sponsors of the exhibition, she introduced Dr. Arlene Dávila, who was the session chairperson.

Dr. Dávila began the proceedings with her paper entitled "Local/ Diasporic Taínos: Towards a Cultural Politics of Memory, Reality, and Imagery." She gave an overview of the use of Taíno imagery and symbolism among Puerto Ricans residing within and outside the island. Dávila noted the persistence of Taíno culture in everyday life, and the increased use of Taíno imagery as a national symbol after the island achieved commonwealth status in 1952. She also noted that historically, Taíno culture has been used as a "lost heritage" in creating and promoting the myth of a harmonious merging of three races in Puerto Rico. Within this context, she also attempted to conceptualize what she referred to as the current Taíno movement or "resurgence," while not asserting the veracity of Taíno survival or Taíno authenticity. I felt this was quite an interesting paradox as Dávila opened her presentation with a description of how she had been questioned about her indigenous ancestry in the past. According to Dr. Dávila, this "link to her Taíno identity" was made not only by a well-known Puerto Rican scholar but also by persons identifying themselves as Taíno. Although she admitted to being uncomfortable with having her Puerto Rican identity questioned outright, she never revealed to the audience what she considered herself to be. It would have been interesting to have heard if her involvement with this issue had invoked any change with regard to her personal understanding or expression of her identity.

Dr. Dávila briefly touched upon the historical continuity of an indigenous presence in Puerto Rico, mentioning a 1778 census which she believed was the last documented evidence of Taíno people as a separate ethnic group in Puerto Rico. As she had noted earlier, her objective was not to authenticate Taíno survival, and so her presentation of Taíno historical continuity was not developed. Instead, Dr. Dávila evaluated the current expressions of Taíno identity in the United States and on the island, asserting that Taíno activists on the mainland have been able to achieve more recognition because of United States policies promoting cultural diversity. In what was to be the most popular theme of the day, Dávila proposed that identifying with the Taíno reflected the inability of Puerto Ricans to deal with the historical legacy of Puerto Rico's African heritage. While it could be argued that her essay promoted a more than skeptical tone toward contemporary Taínos, Dr. Dávila must be cited for being the only presenter to actually interview Taíno people for her presentation.

While the academic credentials of the other panelist were impressive, the subject matter explored in their papers also seemed to transmit an anti-Taíno sentiment. This observation was voiced by quite a number of people from the audience during the question-and-answer period that followed. The essays included catchy titles like "Making Indians out of Blacks: The Revitalization of Taíno Identity in Contemporary Puerto Rico," "What's in a name, an Indian name?," and "The Indians are Coming, the Indians Are Coming—Becoming Taíno in the 21st Century." Perhaps unintentionally, these presentations perpetuated the same historical misconceptions that these scholars were attempting to reevaluate. What was therefore suggested to the audience were the very same Eurocentric assumptions that contemporary Taíno activists have been working so hard to change.

The next panelist was Dr. Jorge Duany of the University of Puerto Rico, whose presentation was titled, "Making Indians out of Blacks: The

Revitalization of Taíno Identity in Contemporary Puerto Rico." Dr. Duany focused on the development of the Taíno as an intellectual discourse. He began by proposing that "nations are engineered communities with invented traditions constructed by politicians and scholars." He then proceeded to discuss the concept of "our Indians," the institutionalization of the Taíno as archeological patrimony, and the many historical "enigmas" that were filled by the speculations of past scholars. Like Dr. Dávila, Duany highlighted the rise of nationalism and the shifts in party politics. He also documented the romantic use of Taíno imagery as a means of resistance against the "Yankee incursion," and he also noted the lack of an African perspective within the programs of the Institute of Puerto Rican Culture. With this in mind, Dr. Duany seemed intent on asserting that the symbolic displacement of the African heritage was a result of the promotion and canonization of the Taíno heritage by Spanish Creoles, who pitted the "subordinate races" against each other. Interestingly, the idea of the Taíno as the "first root" of the mythical Puerto Rican racial triad or hierarchy was also down played by Duany as well as by the other panelists. This was something I found disturbing because, regardless of what the scholars were attempting to prove, the simple fact remains that the Taínos were on the islands before the arrival of the Europeans and the enslaved Africans who were brought to the Caribbean during the Spanish colonial period.

Dr. Duany's dismissive attitude toward the contemporary Taíno movement was revealed when he stated, "I don't know what is happening as far as the Taíno movement in New York is concerned, so I will only speak about Puerto Rico." Duany also said that the Taíno movement in contemporary Puerto Rico has been relatively unimportant and has had little or no impact. While listening to this, I could not help but feel that the lack of research and outright denial of Puerto Rico's Taíno "phenomenon" by this island-based scholar exhibited the contempt that most academics have towards Taíno/Indigenous affirmation in general. It is well documented that persons asserting their Taíno identity have been quite active in Puerto Rico in recent years. I personally have participated in many Taíno-related activities in Puerto Rico and throughout the Caribbean. Although at first glance, the indigenous movement in Puerto Rico may not appear to be as boisterous as it is in the United States, there have been a number of newspaper articles, radio interviews, and even local television interviews, which have presented contemporary Taíno activists to the Puerto Rican public. Whether or not the majority of Puerto Ricans have accepted them as Taíno is another story. The activities of Elba Lugo, Paseo Taíno and the Consejo General de Taínos Borincanos, Naniki Reyes Ocasio and the Caney Quinto Mundo, and even the humble Cheverez Family of Morovis were not even mentioned by Duany.[2] One would have thought that Dr. Duany might have interviewed some of these well-known island residents, since as the title of his paper suggest, he was to have spoken on the revitalization of Taíno identity in contemporary Puerto Rico.

It was Dr. Peter Roberts of the University of the West Indies at Cave Hill who presented the next paper, entitled "What's in a name, an Indian name?" Dr. Roberts immediately distinguished himself from the other panelists by stating he was neither a Puerto Rican nor a Hispanic. At this point, after having suffered through the "Puerto Rican" perspectives of the previous panelists, I was looking forward to a different and perhaps unbiased discourse. As a Black academic, Dr. Roberts was in a unique position to enlighten the audience on issues of identity, not only for Blacks in the English-speaking Caribbean, but also for the contemporary Carib Indian communities of the Lesser Antilles. These indigenous communities, located on islands such as St. Vincent, Dominica, and Trinidad, are also dealing with questions of identity that would have added important comparative information to the discussion;[3] however, Dr. Roberts failed to address these issues. Instead, he focused his discussion on the "fascination with being Indian" asserting that "names do matter"—at least in the Caribbean.

It was Dr. Roberts' contention that meaning was an important factor in the choice of a name, especially an Indian name. Citing the predicament of Romeo and Juliet in Shakespeare's play, Dr. Roberts suggested that a choice of a name could be used to overcome the specific circumstances of one's birth. He noted that this was true especially in the Caribbean, where name transference has had a long and well-documented history. Dr. Roberts explained that in the English-speaking Caribbean, the negative or positive values of society were acted out through Indian names, and other terminology or imagery. His first example was the European use of the word "Indian" in the sixteenth century and its application to both Native Americans and the populations of the Indian subcontinent. He then turned his attention to the development of the racial categories in the Dominican Republic. Roberts referred to the term *"Indio,"* which has been used to classify Blacks and mulattos in that country. Dr. Roberts noted that the term "Indian" was used not only to differentiate Dominicans from their Black Haitian neighbors, but also to make Dominicans acceptable to the "White Nations." With this in mind, Roberts asserted that the term Indian is now used universally to define three racial types—Native Americans, people from the Indian subcontinent, and Blacks in the Dominican Republic who are not Haitians.

Dr. Roberts also cited the use of the term "Carib" as another example of name transference in the Caribbean. According to Roberts, this term is used to describe another Caribbean indigenous ethnic group who inhabited the Lesser Antilles. Dr. Roberts pointed out that the Carib have been historically depicted as fierce man-eaters in contrast to the Taíno, who have been portrayed as docile, friendly, peaceful and therefore easily subjugated. This view of the Taíno, which has been connected to the concept of the "noble savage," was also brought up by another panelist. Unfortunately, none of the presenters developed this concept or the concept of the "good" and "bad Indian" and its significance. For example, several scholars have conceded that there is no verifiable evidence to prove that the Caribs, were cannibals.[4] Yet this portrayal of the so-called Caribs was essential to the success of early European colonization because royal decrees made it unlawful to enslave "good Indians" or *"Guatiaos"* as Roberts called them. For the profit-motivated colonizers, it was necessary to establish that most Indians were evil, idolatrous cannibals. In this way it was legal for them to be enslaved. This scenario was used most notably in the Spanish campaigns against the Indigenous Peoples of Mexico, especially the Maya,[5] but it began with the Taíno in the Caribbean. As Dr. Roberts described it, the term *Guatiao* and the ceremony it described, originated with the Taíno, who developed and implemented this social, political, and religious concept through the exchange of names and a bond of friendship. With the establishment of this reciprocal relationship, the *Guatiao* ceremony was ultimately geared toward building good trade relations among the Taíno and other peoples. Roberts also noted that the Taíno used the *Guatiao* ceremony to adopt the Spaniards in the early stages of the colonization process.

It was at this point in his presentation that Dr. Roberts drew attention to the term *"guajiro,"* which he defined as an Amerindian word from Venezuela that had been "transferred" to the rural community of Cuba. He then discussed the rise of Cuban "Ciboneyismo," which was a movement that fostered Cuban national pride in reaction to Spanish colonialism.[6] Roberts noted that it was the Spanish who first attempted to rank persons by race or race mixture. In this mathematical exercise, individuals were identified by the "amounts of blood" (i.e., skin color) that people had, and this in turn determined privilege and social status. This ranking system was also instituted in the British colony of Jamaica, where color became a major factor in what Roberts described as "a linear ascent to becoming White."

Ms. Miriam Jiménez Román, a New York–based independent scholar, presented the final symposium paper entitled, "The Indians are Coming, the Indians are Coming—Becoming Taíno in the 21st Century." Ms. Jiménez immediately struck me as a most unfortunate choice for a panelist because she openly admitted in the beginning of her discourse that she had done no previous research on the Taíno, focusing instead on the general issue of race in Puerto Rico. Curiously, Ms. Jiménez did not offer any information about the specifics of her research on race, but it was clear that it did not include research on the indigenous element in Puerto Rico. I felt that this would have been a good opportunity for the organizers of the panel session to include a Taíno activist who could have discussed the Indigenous Peoples of the contemporary Caribbean and their perspectives on identity. Regrettably, because the symposium focused on an intellectual discourse by academics, it followed the same flawed format as previous panels hosted by El Museo del Barrio on the Taíno Legacy. The failure to include Taíno activists as equal participants in all of the panel discussions and in the publications that focused on issues of concern to Taínos was symptomatic of the attitude that prevailed among exhibit and symposium organizers.[7]

Ms. Jiménez began her presentation with an overview of the situation of Native Peoples in the United States. She highlighted the fact that the identification of who was an "Indian" was at one time determined solely by the "tribes" themselves. She also discussed the complex issue of indigenous identity based on "blood quantum" as opposed to "self-identification." Citing a statement by a Native American opposed to self-identification, Ms. Jiménez drew attention to the very large number of persons who claim part-Cherokee ancestry. She also noted the recent shift in United States policy with regard to the official recognition of Native Americans, which now emphasizes biological proof of origin, as opposed to self-identification. Ms. Jiménez attributed the shift in policy to a "legitimacy factor" that arose from disputes over land rights and sovereignty issues. It was here that she made reference to the court cases that involved the Ramapough people of New Jersey and the Mashantucket Pequots of Connecticut. Both of these groups retain little of their ancestral culture, have suffered language loss, and are biologically "mixed" as well. Nevertheless, the Mashantucket Peqouts were able to gain official recognition by the federal government as a tribe due to family documents and the demonstration of "verifiable" blood ties to "full-blooded" ancestors. According to Ms. Jiménez, the Peqouts currently run the nation's most profitable casino and can afford to hire anthropologists to assist them with their cultural reaffirmation.

It was at this point that Ms. Jiménez could have focused on the reality of the Peqouts, Ramapoughs, and other East Coast Indigenous Peoples identified as tri-racial isolates. This is an important observation that should have been developed to further impress upon the audience the similarity in the circumstances of these North American Indian groups to the current situation facing the Taíno People. For instance, and as stated by Jiménez, these groups have not retained much in the way of cultural or linguistic continuity. If she had been more objective on this subject she might have conceded that in many instances, although historically not recognized as a separate ethnic group, Caribbean peoples retain much more of their indigenous cultural and linguistic characteristics than do many Indigenous communities in eastern North America. Rather than her disavowing Taíno affirmation, she could have used this link to present at least the possibility of a Taíno reality. However, it appears that Ms. Jiménez accepts the very same polemic she described and denounced in another context: the promotion of the North American Plains Indian as the archetype for "Indianess." Indeed, the appropriation of this ideology can clearly be seen in contemporary Caribbean cultural displays, such as in carnivals and *botanicas*, and in religious practices, such as Santería. As noted by Ms.

Jiménez, these Caribbean cultural expressions which continuously exploit the "mythical" plains Indian image as the only "true Indian" have long since been imposed upon the psyche of Latin Americans. It is lamentable that Ms. Jiménez did not focus more intently on this particular topic. Perhaps if she had, the Puerto Ricans and other Latin Americans attending this symposium might have been able to put this issue into some context—for example, by connecting their own experiences with the indigenous reality of the Caribbean. Instead, Ms. Jiménez maintained the same tired rhetoric as did the previous presenters—the promotion of the Taíno as the "evasion of Blackness."

While I agree with Ms. Jiménez and the other panelists that there is definitely racial prejudice towards Blacks in the Greater Antilles, the problem is that these scholars have transposed the "Black Experience" of the United States to Puerto Rico and other parts of the Caribbean. This afrocentric propaganda has served to perpetuate the idea that race relations among Puerto Ricans is simply a "Black and White" issue—totally disregarding even the remote possibility of other realities. The presentation of these uncontested academic viewpoints is no different than what Ms. Jiménez described as the use of the Taíno to construct a direct "path to Whiteness."

From what I could discern, it appears that Ms. Jiménez would like to see Puerto Ricans construct a "path to Blackness." The views presented by the other panelists also seemed to support this rhetoric as well. What is most alarming to me is that these scholarly positions could be easily regarded as infallible by a public eager for some clarity on the complex issue of identity for Puerto Ricans and other Latinos. This was most evident to me during the question and answer period when a young Puerto Rican male asked the panelists in almost desperation and anger, "What am I, Black, White or Indian? I want to know."

With academics articulating only what they feel is appropriate and in line with current trends, they are simply continuing an agenda that has been institutionalized throughout the Americas since the first days of the European colonization. Current trendy ideas include the myth of Taíno extinction, and the fanciful view that Puerto Ricans are both a nationality and a race. Yet another concept that continues to be popular up to the present time is the almost religious devotion to the myth portraying

Christopher Columbus as a hero. All persons of good conscience should be aware that there is an overwhelming amount of evidence that confirms that glorifying Columbus, the "Christ-bearing colonizer," is not only politically incorrect, but also morally incorrect. For the Indigenous Peoples of this hemisphere, and African peoples as well, Columbus remains the ultimate symbol of racism, genocide, and colonialism. In spite of this knowledge, Columbus Day is still celebrated throughout the United States, Puerto Rico, and the Caribbean.

As Ms. Jiménez continued her presentation, her attention turned towards her recent experiences with the contemporary Taíno. Her generally sarcastic tone made it clear that as far as she was concerned, her judgement on the Taíno movement was complete and that her personal feelings could not afford an objective analysis. As she described her visit to the Internet Websites of two Taíno organizations,[8] one could almost feel her pain, which seemed to be the result of a questioning of her seemingly comfortable identity as a Puerto Rican. This was evident to me in statements like "…because these organizations require a photo…would I fit the criteria to be included in this Taíno registry?" It was quite obvious that as far as she was concerned, she would not fit the criteria for "Indianess" and would not be accepted as Taíno.

It was at this point in her discourse that Ms. Jiménez made the incredible determination that the Taíno organizations and their procedures could be compared to the oppressive pre-Mandela apartheid regime in South Africa. I found it rather strange that Ms. Jiménez would present her unanswered questions about the criteria for being a Taíno to this particular audience without having previously approached the Taíno organizations themselves. I brought this fact to the attention of Ms. Jiménez during the question-and-answer period that followed. While I am not a college-educated person, simple logic would dictate that in order to get a better understanding of an organization's membership procedures and philosophy, one should come into direct contact with the organization in question. For Ms. Jiménez, this would not have required much research because the phone numbers, e-mail and postal addresses of the groups are available on the web pages that she said she visited. Once again, with the exception of Dr. Dávila, not one of the panelists interviewed any contemporary Taíno people for their presentations. This was the case even though the panelists were well aware of the existence of individuals and organizations identifying themselves as Taíno.

In what seemed to me to be an attempt to gain the sympathy of Puerto Rican nationalists, Ms. Jiménez spoke of the divisiveness of creating a "nation within a nation." Now on the offensive, she said the following almost defiantly: "…am I now to understand that as a Puerto Rican, I am denying the rights of Taínos, who are doubly colonized?" She also had no qualms about suggesting that the Taíno movement was motivated by a profit or funding incentive. To substantiate her claims, she made reference to the current availability of Taíno items that are for sale through the Internet. But as one might have guessed, she did not offer a comparison or even mention the many stylistically African items on sale via the Internet or at boutiques and botanicas throughout the United States and the Caribbean.

Obviously seeking to discredit the Taíno movement, Ms. Jiménez focused on the Internet statement of an individual Taíno who claimed ancestry from a specific Cacique or chieftain. She then described the difficulty that Puerto Ricans have in tracing their ancestry and noted that "most Puerto Ricans can't remember their great-grandfather" and that "Puerto Rico does not have this type of genealogical documentation." This was a very careless and misleading statement, as representatives of the various Puerto Rican genealogical societies would note. Although genealogical records in Puerto Rico were not maintained with the same care as in the United States, records do indeed exist in the form of censuses, surveys, and reports. The Spaniards also keep census records and other data, and although many of the original documents have either been lost or are kept in Spain, a number of Puerto Rican historians have noted their existence.[9] Reference should also be made to the Puerto Rican municipalities and churches that have also kept some records of births and deaths as well as baptismal papers.

As the final presentation concluded and the stage was being prepared for the question-and-answer period, I could feel the tension and confusion that permeated the air. The presenters seemed fully prepared to speak before a group of academics, but it was clear that they had little or no connection with the mostly community-based audience and their views on the topic. Perhaps if the academic discourse on Taíno "revitalization" had attempted to objectively emphasize the current grass roots activism, a less antagonistic dialogue between the presenters and the audience might have occurred.

As I looked at my notes, it seemed as if all the presenters were intent on suggesting that the assertion of anything Taíno was simply a way for Puerto Ricans to deny or separate themselves from their African heritage. While the entire panel denounced the attempts to "whiten" Puerto Rican or Caribbean society, the alternative that they offered reduced everything to a purely "Black and White" issue. For these scholars there was no exploration of the middle ground, nor was there even the remote possibility that an indigenous reality could be considered. One could have easily left this symposium erroneously concluding that practically every Puerto Rican can claim Taíno ancestry, but as the *"color canela"* slowly dilutes away physically and mentally, a true Puerto Rican or Latino/Hispano is ultimately White or Black. As I had stated earlier, I was not the only person who was left with this impression. It was clearly demonstrated during the question-and-answer period that followed.

Roger Hernandez, who identified himself as a "Taíno from the neighborhood," made the first comment from the floor. He told the scholars that although he was born in New York, there might be some who would not accept him as a New Yorker. He also noted that the panelists were free to decide what he might be, but that his own people accepted him as Taíno and that was good enough for him. In response to this statement Dr. Peter Roberts replied: "Why do you call yourself a Taíno when you are a mixture? Why are you focusing on the Taíno only?" I found this reply a little disconcerting and wondered how Dr. Roberts would feel if someone had asked him a similar question. I also wondered when this "educated man" last thought about his own identity, particularly since many persons of African descent in the Caribbean are a "mixture" and retain Caucasian as well as Indigenous ancestry. Overall, it appeared that Dr. Roberts and the other panelists were suggesting that if persons exhibit African physical traits, no one questions their African ancestry or their "degree of Blackness" regardless of their skin color—unless they are obviously white. This assumption and the overall attitude of the panelists leaves one with the absurd impression that it only takes a little African blood to make a person Black, but it takes a whole lot of Indian blood to make a real Indian.

Continuing on this theme, another member of the audience noted certain comments made by the scholars suggesting that there has been no movement of African consciousness in Puerto Rico that could compare to the current movement for Taíno reaffirmation. This person asked if it was not the responsibility of the academic community to address and clarify this issue through proper education. After the symposium, I was also told that it felt as if the scholars were blaming the Taíno for something that should ultimately be decided by the Black community, and that the panelists might be suggesting that there was not a Black reality in Puerto Rico.

Instead of pitting the races against each other, this discussion of identity and cultural reaffirmation could have been developed by the scholars into a more objective symposium, emphasizing the current revitalization of both the Taíno and African heritage. For instance, there are millions of people of African descent throughout the Americas, and with very few exceptions, most have lost their understanding of ancestral languages, genealogy, religions, customs, and tribal identity. Despite these facts, there has been an undeniable rise in the exploration and reaffirmation of African culture and heritage. The establishment of the African-American holiday of Kwanzaa is a clear example of this trend. Many Blacks are also reconnecting to their roots by traveling back to Africa, even though the overwhelming majority of Blacks do not know from what area their ancestors came from. Today, it is not uncommon for Blacks to wear traditional styles of African dress in an effort to rebuild their ancestral connections and instill pride and self-esteem within their communities. For the most part, these noble efforts have not been condemned by scholars and intellectuals, but rather applauded. It is distressing to note that Indigenous Peoples like the Taíno, who are going through a similar process, are not congratulated on these same initiatives but are subjected to ridicule. It is no wonder that members of the audience kept remarking on the antagonistic attitudes of the panelists toward the Taíno movement. As the audience critique continued, the academics were noticeably shaken—seemingly unprepared for an assault on their hegemonic points of view.

In another comment from the audience, it was noted that the presenters would suggest to an unsuspecting audience that the Taíno "revival" movement is an isolated "phenomenon" limited to Puerto Ricans, while arrogantly ignoring the activities of other Taíno/Indigenous descendants throughout the Caribbean. The panelists responded to this by stating that they were only presenting examples of Taíno appropriation for use as a symbol of nationalism among Puerto Ricans, and that their discourse was not meant to answer all the questions, but just begin a dialogue. Continuing on this theme, another person noted that the panelists seemed to separate what was happening in Puerto Rico from what was happening in New York and connected the "New York Taínos" to the "New Age" movement. The lack of scholarly focus on documented connections among and between Taínos and other Indigenous Peoples continues to limit public awareness of this issue. Reminiscent of the divide-and-conquer strategy once used by the conquistadors, this manipulative approach on the part of the scholars has become institutionalized in the educational systems of the Americas.

It must be noted that this attempt to separate the Taíno from other Indigenous People is nothing new in the scholarly discourse. The evolutionary origins of the Taíno have been consistently presented in isolation from the experiences of other Indigenous Peoples by Caribbean scholars, such as Dr. Ricardo Alegría of the Institute of Puerto Rican Culture, and Dr. Irving Rouse of Yale University. Although there has been ample evidence to indicate that the development of the Taíno as a particular ethnic group was not confined to the Arawak origins of South America, direct cultural, linguistic, and archeological ties to Mesoamerica and the mainland of the United States have been deliberately ignored.[10] As a result of the imposed isolation theories, the current discussion of Taíno affirmation is not viewed in the broader context of the continental Indigenous movement for civil rights that began at the beginning of the 1970s. In the Caribbean and the United States, there is documentation that individuals and groups were active in promoting Taíno culture as a living heritage in that time period.[11] Even earlier, in the late 1800s and early 1900s, institutions like the Smithsonian's National Museum of the American Indian and the U.S. War Department had separately documented the survival of Taíno descendants in Cuba and Puerto Rico.[12] Although today's anthropologists might look down on the type of physical anthropology that was used at that time, it nevertheless indicates a physical continuity and reality that in fact continues up until the present time.

At certain points during the course of the discussion, the panelists expressed their concern about the apparent importance that the Taíno of the contemporary period place on physical appearance. They described a much-coveted "Taíno look" or phenotype as the traditional "Indian" stereotype of high cheekbones, copper skin, and straight black hair. It was Dr. Duany who made reference to a study that was done at the University of Puerto Rico in the 1970s, which concluded that over 30 percent of the students exhibited biological traits attributed to Indigenous Peoples. However, it was also Dr. Duany who said that he teaches "at the University of Puerto Rico, and I don't see where this comes from." Consciously or unconsciously, what Dr. Duany failed to mention was that a particular tooth formation known as "Diente de Pala" or "Shovel Teeth" and a specific blood type common to Native Americans, served as a basis for this study.[13] Since he admitted that he knew this, it was difficult to determine what he was looking for when he claimed he could not see indigenous traits in his own students. It would seem that Dr. Duany was measuring the indigenous authenticity of his students according to the same physical stereotype that he and the other panelists claimed the Taíno activists were guilty of emulating.

In this or any discussion of color, race, or any other issue concerning Taíno identity, what is of great concern to me is that the subjects in question are addressed from a Taíno perspective. Although some may argue that current Taíno perspectives are not verifiable, we can cautiously review the available historical data and come to a reasonably accurate conclusion. As I had suggested earlier, not addressing the historical continuity of Taíno survival in this discussion was where the panelist made a serious mistake, for without this information, the Taíno cannot be discussed objectively. It was Dr. Roberts who mentioned that the sacred ceremony of *Guatiao* was used by the Taíno to adopt Spaniards, but neither he nor the other panelists recognized the important implications of this practice. If the Taíno could adopt the White Spaniard or even the Black Africans who escaped into the mountains and joined the Taíno communities—then it becomes clear to me what the Taíno stance on color and race would be. To further illustrate the Taíno view on this issue, let us review a statement made by Cardinal Cisneros in 1516. The Cardinal had instructed three Hieronymite monks who were being sent to the Indies to advise Spanish men to marry their Indian mistresses, especially if they were the daughters of a *Cacique* or chieftain.[14] Potentially, what this meant in practice was that if the *Cacique* failed to have a son, the Spaniard would become the *Cacique* through marriage, which also gives us another perspective on the Taíno view towards race relations.

As I continued to listen to the comments of my "colleagues" in the audience, I could not help but think of all the Indigenous Peoples who have gone through a process of mental abuse, physical exploitation, and genocide, and why many of them deny their heritage. At that moment I could only be thankful that it was my own mother who first told me of my Indian heritage, and even though she thought that her knowledge was insufficient, these "seeds of identity" were very important and certainly more than what other people have received.

The denial of an indigenous heritage was yet another substantive issue that the panelists did not consider in the discussion. For example, there was a failure to address the fact that thousands of Native Americans have denied their heritage because within the now dominant Eurocentric or Western milieu, Indigenous Peoples have been traditionally seen as the lowest possible class of people. In Latin America in particular, the Indian has been consistently viewed as the "country bumpkin" and the ultimate representation of the region's lack of progress. This view has long been imposed upon the rural communities of the Greater Antilles, which is precisely where the Taínos have maintained some of the most important aspects of their indigenous heritage. Concerning the Jíbaro or rural folk of Puerto Rico, an officer of the U.S. Army of occupation stated in 1899 that "Like the Indian, the Jíbaro is not given to labor" and "in his resistance to civilization he confines his efforts to the strictest necessities."[15]

Although this legacy of shame and denial of an indigenous identity was not addressed by the panel, families and individuals throughout the Caribbean and the United States have discussed this problem verbally. In the Spanish-speaking Caribbean in particular, many people who are well aware of their Taíno heritage through oral tradition were told as children not to talk about their identity.[16] In fact, a powerful statement made from the floor reflected this sentiment. Vanessa Inarunikia Pastrana, identifying herself as a "proud Taíno woman," informed the panelists that she was born and grew up in the Puerto Rican "*campo*" where she learned the facts of her Indigenous heritage from family members and not from books. She also added that her family was reluctant or did not talk about their Taíno origins in public. Other people have also commented that, in the past, the fear of religious intolerance was also a factor that compelled Indigenous People to "hide" their identity because of its link to non-Christian practices, which was seen as potentially troublesome and even dangerous.

The role that Christian religion played in transforming indigenous reality was also questioned, but this important subject affecting people's identity was also not addressed by any of the panelists. It is well documented that the influence of religion has had devastating effects on indigenous cultures and that this is no less true for the Indigenous Peoples of the Caribbean. What is interesting to note is that despite these adverse effects, elements of indigenous spirituality still permeate Caribbean life and are now being accessed by various communities, groups and individuals. Many of these traditions, which are passed on orally, have taken new precedence, particularly in the case of herbal medicines.[17] As pharmaceutical companies discover the value of the botanical cures in the Amazon and other areas, ancient indigenous practices throughout the hemisphere are gaining credibility and have sparked a resurgence that coincides and compliments the current worldwide emergence of the indigenous rights movement.

The fact that the panelists chose not to address pertinent issues such as historical continuity, self-esteem, religion, comparison with neighboring indigenous communities, and grassroots activism (etc.), should indicate an urgent need to revisit some old questions. For future generations, we need to identify those individuals who are making decisions about identity and values in society and ascertain their ulterior motives. Educators who remain stuck in the same educational systems that have promoted past colonial government policies, will remain in opposition to alternative viewpoints and teaching methods – especially those that are based on indigenous ideology and spirituality. As the recipients of the "fruits" of this type of education, we must come to the realization that these very policies were created under the assumption that the indigenous way of life would soon disappear through integration and assimilation by the dominant culture. Historically speaking, this is precisely why nation-states have not tolerated the assertion of indigenous identity through language or indigenous-controlled education.[18]

Bearing this in mind, we must remind ourselves that these colonial government policies, which have given birth to our present educational system, were transplanted from Europe during the time of the Inquisition. Beginning with Christopher Columbus, politicians, intellectuals and religious advocates came to this hemisphere armed with the ideology of "man over nature" and "man (the European man)" as divine. In a relatively short time, this Eurocentric philosophy, which is now imposed on our present "reality," practically destroyed all spirituality—reducing the earth and all life to nothing more than material resources that can now be used only for scientific and monetary value. By taking the sacredness out of life, we are now confronted by situations where, for the sake of science, we interrupt the eternal rest of our ancestors and display their bones like trophies under glass cases in museums. The use of this scientific inquiry and methodology can never positively analyze any indigenous philosophy or reality, in the past or in the present. This method, which focuses on division and isolation, is in direct conflict with the holistic approach of the indigenous way of life. We, therefore, cannot enter into a discussion of Taíno identity without addressing and incorporating the indigenous perspective into the dialogue. Furthermore, the lack of a formal education must not be a stumbling block for dialogue, and education must not remain an elitist exercise. I am reminded of all the *campesino* (rural) parents and grandparents who sent their children to school with the seeds of an Indian identity, only to have these children return to their homes upset, confused, and disillusioned because their teachers told them that Indians were worthless ignorant savages, or non-existent. This is a mindset that we ourselves promote by continually exalting intellectuals who have perpetuated the colonial status quo throughout Latin America, which retains a racial hierarchy even though skin colors have become blurred.

Although it would seem that Latin American society is a "creature of habit suffering from a battered wife syndrome," we have entered an era where human rights has emerged as a universal concept. Today, the fate of human beings is no longer the prerogative of absolute state power. As access to information increases, so do the opportunities to participate in the process of self-determination. Affirming that self-determination is one of the most important human activities, the United Nations included a provision that supported this principle as a main objective of its original 1945 Charter.[19] In fact, United Nations resolution 1514 (XV) of 14 December 1960 contained a "Declaration on the Granting of Independence to Colonial Countries and Peoples," which stated in part that "All peoples have the right to self-determination" and that "by virtue of that right, they freely determine their political status and freely pursue their economic, social, and cultural development."[20] More recently, at the 1995 International Networking Conference in Honolulu, Scott Crawford and Kelula Bray-Crawford, representing the Nation of Hawai'i, said that "Self-determination is tied-in with all aspects of life—political, economic, and cultural—and is ultimately about how we chose to live, and allow others to live together on this planet."[21]

Recent programs and initiatives by the United Nations indicate that Indigenous Peoples are well aware of this dynamic. The result has been an increased activism of Indigenous Peoples demanding recognition of their basic human rights throughout the world. Indeed, the United Nations Economic and Social Council created the Working Group on Indigenous Populations in 1982, and it has continuously exemplified this increased activism in recent years. In 1985, the Working Group began preparing a draft Declaration on the Rights of Indigenous Peoples, and in 1993, its final text was completed. This document now represents one of the most important developments in the promotion and protection of the basic rights and fundamental freedoms of Indigenous Peoples. Some of the rights identified within the document include the right to an identity, the right to have a language, the protection of intellectual and cultural property and the right to self-determination. Taíno affirmation must be viewed within this context, and all sectors of Caribbean society must acknowledge that asserting self-determination is a basic human right of all peoples, including the Taíno People.

Although this symposium was probably one of the more emotionally charged events of the exhibit on Taíno Art and Culture, I remain appreciative that these scholars took time out from their busy schedules to share their views with a public eager for dialogue on this subject. It is my hope that the scholars also appreciate the participation of the many people from diverse backgrounds who also gave of their time to share in this precedent-setting experience. I also would like to personally commend the initiative that was taken by El Museo del Barrio, not only in hosting this symposium, but also for including the Taíno Legacy portion with the exhibition.

It is important to also acknowledge the support and positive participation of the Taíno organizations that had representatives in attendance at this symposium. These organizations included the Consejo General de Taínos Borincanos, Cacibajagua, Presencia Taína, and the Maisiti Yucayeque Taíno. I also want to express my gratitude to Dr. Gabriel Haslip-Viera, acting director of the Center for Puerto Rican Studies at Hunter College in New York, for his inspiration and invitation to expand upon my previous article and to share my perspectives as a proud Taíno man.

Notes

1. Roberto Borrero, "Symposium: Rethinking Taíno—The Cultural Politics of the use of Their Imagery," *La Voz del Pueblo Taíno*, vol. 1, issue 3 (May 1998), p. 5.

2. Elba Lugo and Paseo Taíno/Travesía Taína appeared in the *Spirits of the Jaguar*, a PBS documentary. They also have organized Taíno cultural presentations at the Tibes and Caguana Ceremonial parks, the University of Puerto Rico, and the Festival Indigena de Jayuya, etc. The Consejo General de Taínos Borincanos has organized environmental "clean-ups" and has been represented at the United Nations. Naniki Reyes Ocasio and the Caney Quinto Mundo have been recognized by Puerto Rico's current governor and maintain a 400-acre land base in Ciales. The Cheverez family was featured in the film *Raices Indigena*.

3. Chief Hillary Fredricks (Carib) of Dominica, personal communication (1998).

4. Kirkpatrick Sale, *The Conquest of Paradise: Christopher Columbus and the Columbian Legacy* (New York: Alfred A. Knopf, 1990), pp. 130–137, and Jalil Sued-Badillo, *Los Caribes: Realidad o Fábula* (Rio Piedras, Puerto Rico: Editorial Antillana, 1978).

5. Yucatan Mayan Elder and Ceremonial Leader, Hunbatz Men—personal communication (1997).

6. "Ciboney" is a term for an aboriginal group native to Cuba and parts of the Dominican Republic. The debate among academics still continues as to whether they were a sub-group of the Taíno or a different ethnic group altogether.

7. During the exhibit's preparatory phase, contemporary Taínos such as myself

were contacted and consulted for input and support. On July 18, 1997, several months before the opening of the exhibit, a group of Taíno activists met at El Museo for a planning session on the "Taíno Legacy Project," which would involve an alternative exhibition and panel discussions to run concurrently with the main exhibit. Unfortunately, the "Taíno Legacy Exhibit" ended sooner than the archaeologically oriented main exhibit, nor did its accompanying publication mention or include any contemporary Taíno viewpoints. Taíno activists were also not afforded ample opportunity to share their viewpoints as equals with the scholars at the various symposia, whose content was planned and organized solely by the staff of El Museo.

8. The Taíno Inter-Tribal Council and the Nación Taína.

9. Salvador Brau, *Puerto Rico y su historia: investigaciones criticas* (Valencia: Imprenta de F. Vives Mora, 1894).

10. Sven Loven, *Origins of Tainan Culture, West Indies* (Goteborg: Elanders Boktryckeri Aktiebolag, 1935), and Eugenio Fernández-Méndez, *Art and Mythology of the Taíno Indian of the Greater Antilles* (San Juan, Puerto Rico: Ediciones El Cemi, 1972).

11. Don Cesar Serraty established Artesanos los Taínos in the Dominican Republic. There is also the long-term activism of Pedro Guanikeyu Torres, and Marie Helen La Raraque—personal communications (1995–1998).

12. Frederick Webb Hodge, *Indian Notes and Monographs—Guide to the collection from the West Indies* (New York: National Museum of the American Indian, Heye Foundation, 1922), and United States War Department, Porto Rico Census Office, *Report on the Census of Porto Rico 1899* (Washington D.C.: U.S. Government Printing Office, 1900), pp. 29–30.

13. Roberto Martínez-Torres, "Nuestros Indios Siguen Vivos," *Archivo Historico de Morovis*, año 1, no.3 (Junio–Julio de 1987), pp. 56–67.

14. Stan Stiener, *The Islands: The Worlds of the Puerto Ricans* (New York: Harper and Row, 1974), p. 31.

15. Stiener 1974, p. 95.

16. Roberto Borrero, "Ciboney Tribe Joins the UCTP," *La Voz del Pueblo Taíno*, vol. 1, issue 6 (1998), p. 3.

17. In the Caribbean, one of the best examples of this practice would be the remarkable advance in traditional and natural medicine, also known as "Green Medicine" in present-day Cuba.

18. Elsa Stamatopoulou, "Indigenous Peoples and the United Nations: Human Rights as a Developing Dynamic," *Human Rights Quarterly*, vol. 16, no.1 (February 1994), p. 65.

19. Charter of the United Nations, San Francisco, 26 June 1945 <gopher:// gopher.undp.org:70/11/unearth>

20. UN General Assembly resolution1 514 (XV), Declaration on the Granting of Independence to Colonial Countries and Peoples, 947th plenary meeting, 14 December 1960. <http:llhawaii-nation.org/nation/1514.html>

21. Scott Crawford and Kelula Crawford, "Self-Determination in the Information Age," <http://www.hawaii-nation.org/>.

Contributors

Arlene Dávila is known for her unique approach to research on Puerto Rican and Latino identity as it relates to media and consumerism. She is the author of *Sponsored Identities: Cultural Politics in Puerto Rico* (1997), and *Latinos, Inc.: The Marketing and Making of a People* (2001). Dr. Dávila is currently an assistant professor of anthropology at New York University.

Jorge Duany teaches anthropology at the Universidad del Sagrado Corazón (University of the Sacred Heart) in Puerto Rico. He is the former editor of *Revista de Ciencias Sociales* (Revie ɔf the Social Sciences), and is co-author (with José Cobas) of *Cubans in Puerto Rico: Ethnic Economy and Cultural Identity* (1997).

Gabriel Haslip-Viera is co-editor of *Latinos in New York: Communities in Transition* (1996) and author of *Crime and Punishment in Late Colonial Mexico City, 1692–1810* (1999). He is currently an associate professor in the Department of Sociology at the City College of the City University of New York, and director of its Program in Latin American and Latino Studies.

Miriam Jiménez Román is an independent scholar and former managing editor of *Centro Journal*, the official publication of the Center for Puerto Rican Studies at Hunter College, the City University of New York. She is known for her research on race and Latino identity, and is the author of "Un hombre (negro) del pueblo: José Celso Barbosa and the Puerto Rican 'Race' Towards Whiteness," which was published in the *Centro Journal* in 1996.

Peter A. Roberts is professor and chair of the Department of Language, Linguistics and Literature at the University of the West Indies, Cave Hill, Barbados. He is the author of *West Indians and*

161

Their Language (1988), and *From Oral to Literate Culture: the Colonial Experience in the British West Indies* (1997).

Roberto Mucaro Borrero is a representative of the United Confederation of Taíno People and has been editor and publisher of *La Voz del Pueblo Taíno* (The Voice of the Taino People), the official publication of the United States Regional Chapter of the United Confederation since 1998. He is currently the Indigenous and Native American Coordinator for Multicultural Programs in the Education Department of the American Museum of Natural History in New York City.

CPSIA information can be obtained
at www.ICGtesting.com
Printed in the USA
LVHW041210130920
665862LV00001B/92

9 781558 762596